WHAT IS SIX SIGMA?

PETE PANDE
LARRY HOLPP

McGraw-Hill

New York Chicago San Francisco Lisbon
London Madrid Mexico City Milan New Delhi
San Juan Seoul Singapore Sydney Toronto

McGraw-Hill

A Division of The McGraw·Hill Companies

8 9 0 AGM/AGM 0 9 8 7 6 5 4 3

ISBN 0-07-138185-6

Printed and bound by Quebecor/World Martinsburg.

McGraw-Hill books are available at special quantity discounts to use as premiums and sales promotions, or for use in corporate training programs. For more information, please write to the Director of Special Sales, Professional Publishing, McGraw-Hill, Two Penn Plaza, New York, NY 10121-2298. Or contact your local bookstore.

Cataloguing-in-Publication Data is on file for this title at the Library of Congress.

To all the many dedicated people—leaders, managers, fellow consultants, and especially those on the front lines of business— who are making Six Sigma work every day.

CONTENTS

ACKNOWLEDGMENTS

If this book succeeds in helping its readers understand and successfully participate in Six Sigma efforts, it's thanks to the work of hundreds of people who have helped us learn and share this "new" (and yet not-so-new) approach to business success.

The foremost recognition goes to Jack Welch, the now-retired chairman of General Electric who challenged his company to revive the supposedly tired concepts of "quality" and turn them into a practical and usable way to think and manage a business. Characteristically, Six Sigma is an example of Mr. Welch's ability to "zig" when others were "zagging." (Now a lot of other people are zigging, too.)

Along with Jack Welch, recognition should go to another corporate leader, Larry Bossidy of Honeywell, who actually influenced and inspired his pal Jack to get Six Sigma started at GE. Mr. Bossidy's Six Sigma leadership is less publicized, but just as important.

All our clients have contributed to this book in ways visible and subtle. At each of these organizations, dozens if not hundreds of people deserve credit. For providing examples and insights, we need to offer special thanks to Starwood Hotels' Barry Sternlicht, Bob Cotter, and James Hyman; Mark Good and Eric Berglind at Sears Roebuck and Co.; Tom Cole, Tom Jones, and Peter Longo at Federated Logistics and Operations; and Marcey Evans and Jim Perozich at Ford Motor Company.

We'd never get anything done without the help of our colleagues at Pivotal Resources, who are in the trenches every day explaining, coaching, and teaching people how to make Six Sigma ideas and tools work to improve profits and customer satisfaction. We would not have had the opportunity to do this book without the efforts of Bob Neuman and Roland Cavanagh, co-authors on two other works on Six Sigma. Essential to giving us the time and energy to put words on paper are Cheralynn Abbott, Carolyn Talasek, Julie Oseland, and Tina Oakley— along with a long list of unsung heros. Thanks to Dodd Starbird for a great project example.

The real driver behind this book has been our editor, Richard Narramore at McGraw-Hill, whose patience and persistence have been diplomatic and dogged. Thanks, Richard.

Finally, we have to thank Olga, Stephanie, and Brian (Pete's wife and kids) and Pam (Larry's wife) who put up with our road warrior work and stress over deadlines. And thanks to Laura and Ashley (Larry's daughters) for allowing him to break in on their IM sessions to send things back and forth to the editors. We hope our love and appreciation is some compensation for their support and sacrifice. (Now if the kids want to know what we do, we can hand them this book!)

CHAPTER 1

THE SIX SIGMA SUCCESS STORY

You may have heard a rumor, or you may have read something in the company newsletter about Black Belt training. You probably thought, "What do martial arts have to do with my job?" Later, during a department meeting, you learned that your group would be part of a companywide effort (every division!) to implement Six Sigma. Your boss also asked for volunteers to be Black Belts. "What is all this about?" you wondered.

A couple of weeks later, everyone in your division was invited to a big kick-off meeting. Lots of slides were shown, and the company president spoke, mentioning GE, Motorola, and one of your company's big competitors. Examples of Six Sigma and how it could help your division/company save money and make customers happier were given. One speaker said that if it could get from 3 sigma to 4 sigma, your division would save $100 million! 100 million? Was he out of his mind?

Your head was reeling. Was Six Sigma a new flavor-of-the-month program? Could it really save so much money? "What is this thing called Six Sigma?" you thought. "Is there something in it for me? Is it something to worry about?"

Over the past few years, more and more employees of companies that have adopted Six Sigma have asked themselves these kinds of questions. A few of these employees have become Black Belts; others have taken on other roles in this dramatic process of organizational change and renewal. For many employees, the transformation has been both personal and professional.

I never dreamed senior management was really going to support our recommendations. But with Six Sigma, and the data we had to back up our project, they had no choice.

—A TEAM MEMBER FROM A MAJOR RETAILER

This book is dedicated to the millions of employees whose firms are adopting Six Sigma methodologies to improve customer satisfaction, work processes, profitability, speed, and efficiencies of all kinds. When word of the plans to adopt Six Sigma first hits the inside grapevine, it can be confusing and even a little scary. This book will help employees at all levels get ahead of the change curve by explaining

- What Six Sigma is and how it works
- The new roles employees play in Six Sigma
- The Six Sigma problem-solving process
- Why Six Sigma is not a flavor-of-the-month management trend
- The impact Six Sigma can have on the bottom line
- How Six Sigma affects jobs
- What a Six Sigma team is and how it operates
- What you need to know to be successful in a Six Sigma team
- How your customers will be affected by Six Sigma

This book is no substitute for working through a Six Sigma project or training to be a Six Sigma team leader (that's what a Black Belt is, by the way). But this book can help prepare, guide, and support any employee who wants to take advantage of the enormous education, experience, leadership, and technical benefits to those who participate in Six Sigma teams.

WHAT EXACTLY IS SIX SIGMA?

Six Sigma is a smarter way to manage a business or a department. Six Sigma puts the customer first and uses *facts* and *data* to drive better solutions.

Six Sigma efforts target three main areas:

- Improving customer satisfaction
- Reducing cycle time
- Reducing defects

Improvements in these areas usually represent dramatic cost savings to businesses, as well as opportunities to retain customers, capture new markets, and build a reputation for top-performing products and services.

Although it involves measuring and analyzing an organization's business processes, Six Sigma is not merely a *quality* initiative; it is a *business* initiative. Achieving the goal of Six Sigma requires more than small, incremental improvements; it requires breakthroughs in every area of an operation. In statistical terms, "reaching Six Sigma" means that your process or product will perform with almost no defects.

But the real message of Six Sigma goes beyond statistics. Six Sigma is a total management commitment and philosophy of excellence, customer focus, process improvement, and the rule of measurement rather than gut feel. Six Sigma is about making every area of the organization better able to meet the changing needs of customers, markets, and technologies—with benefits for employees, customers, and shareholders.

Six Sigma didn't spring up overnight. Its background stretches back eighty-plus years, from management science concepts developed in the United States to Japanese management breakthroughs to "Total Quality" efforts in the 1970s and 1980s. But its real impact can be seen in the waves of change and positive results sweeping such companies as GE, Motorola, Johnson & Johnson, and American Express.

WHAT'S NEW ABOUT SIX SIGMA?

In the 1980s, Total Quality Management (TQM) was popular. It too was an improvement-focused program, but it ultimately died a slow and silent death in many companies. What makes Six Sigma different?

Three key characteristic separate Six Sigma from quality programs of the past.

1. *Six Sigma is customer focused.* It's almost an obsession to keep external customer needs in plain sight, driving the improvement effort. (External customers are mostly those who buy your business's products and services.)

2. *Six Sigma projects produce major returns on investment.* At GE, for example, the Six Sigma program resulted in the following cost versus returns:

   - In 1996, costs of $200 million and returns of $150 million
   - In 1997, costs of $400 million and returns of $600 million
   - In 1998, costs of $400 million and returns of more than $1 billion

   GE's CEO, Jack Welch, wrote in the annual report that in just three years, Six Sigma had saved the company more than $2 billion.

   We didn't invent Six Sigma—we learned it. The cumulative impact on the company's numbers is not anecdotal, nor a product of charts. It is the product of 276,000 people executing and delivering the result of Six Sigma to our bottom line.

   —JACK WELCH IN 1997

3. *Six Sigma changes how management operates.* Six Sigma is much more than improvement projects. Senior executives and leaders throughout a business are learning the tools and concepts of Six Sigma: new approaches to thinking, planning, and executing to achieve results. In a lot of ways, Six Sigma is about putting into practice the notions of working smarter, not harder.

As we've seen, Six Sigma has produced some impressive numbers. But reaching them requires a great deal of organizational teamwork. It means having the systems to provide customers what they want when they want it. It means providing employees with the time and training to tackle work challenges with some basic, and some sophisticated, analytical tools.

In this short book, we want to give you a feel for Six Sigma without inundating you with facts and details. Our purpose here is not to turn you into a Six Sigma expert but to give you enough information to allow you to draw your own conclusions about what Six Sigma may hold for you personally, for your job, and for your company. Thus prepared, you can decide how you want to get involved and what role you wish to play when Six Sigma comes to your organization. Assuming that you do get involved, you'll understand how to be more effective in making Six Sigma work for you and your business!

CHAPTER 2

SIX WHAT?
WHAT'S A SIGMA?

Understanding Six Sigma does not require any great skill or background in statistics. In fact, "What is Six Sigma" can be answered in various ways. In this chapter, we'll concentrate on defining Six Sigma as

1. A statistical *measure* of the performance of a process or a product
2. A *goal* that reaches near perfection for performance improvement
3. A *system of management* to achieve lasting business leadership and world-class performance

In exploring these definitions, we'll provide some insights into why Six Sigma is such a powerful movement.

SIX SIGMA AS A STATISTICAL MEASURE

If you haven't heard the term "sigma" before, don't worry. Until recently, the term has not been used much in ordinary conversation. The lowercase Greek letter sigma—σ—stands for standard deviation.

Standard deviation is a statistical way to describe how much variation exists in a set of data, a group of items, or a process. For example, if you weigh potato chips of many different sizes, you'll get a higher standard deviation than if you weigh potato chips of all the same size.

As another example, suppose that you run a business that delivers pizzas to nearby offices. You make pretty good pizzas and have lots of customers.

According to your contract with your customers, pizzas will be delivered fresh and hot between 11:45 a.m. and 12:15 p.m. This allows customers to get their orders in time for lunch (their "requirement"). You have also agreed that if a pizza is delivered before 11:45 or after 12:15 (a "defect"), you will discount their next order by 50 percent. Because you and your staff people get a bonus for on-time delivery, you are all very motivated to deliver the pizzas during the half-hour window the customers want.

Here's how Six Sigma, as a measure, could play a part in this simple process: If you deliver only about 68 percent of your pizzas on time, your process is at only a "2 sigma" level. If you deliver 93 percent on time, which sounds good, you are operating at only a "3 sigma" level of performance. If you get 99.4 percent of them there on time, you're operating at "4 sigma."

To be a Six Sigma pizza shop, you would have to have on-time pizza delivery 99.9997 percent of the time! That's practically perfect. In fact, for every million pizzas you make (a lotta mozzarella), you'd end up with only three or four late deliveries. Nice going! (See Figure 2-1 and 2-2.)

Keep in mind that the sigma measure is looking at how well you're meeting customer requirements. If your customers require their pizzas in a 10-minute window, from 11:55 a.m. to 12:05 p.m., your sigma level would almost certainly get worse.

The sigma measure was developed to help:

1. Focus measures on the paying customers of a business. Many of the measures, such as labor hours, costs, and sales volume, companies have traditionally used evaluate things that are not related to what the customer really cares about.

2. Provide a consistent way to measure and to compare different processes. Using the sigma scale, we could assess and compare performance of, say, the pizza baking process with the pizza delivery process—two very different but critical activities.

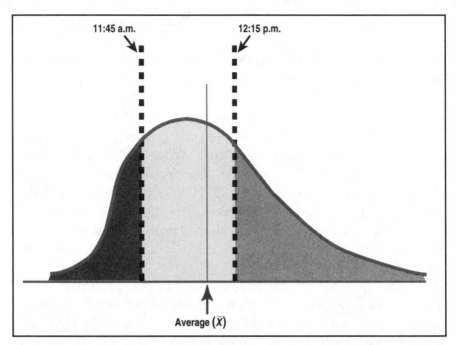

FIGURE 2-1. Variation in pizza delivery 1. With lots of variation, many pizzas arrive early and many arrive late (dark shaded areas). Average delivery is still within the customer requirements (delivery between 11:45 a.m. and 12:45 p.m.). Low "Sigma" score.

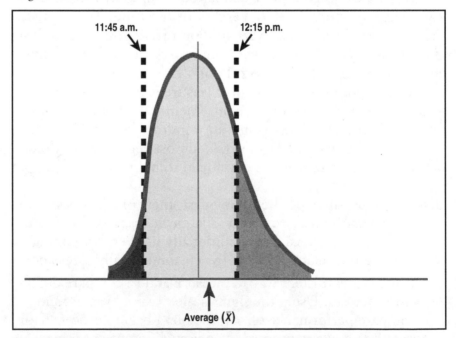

FIGURE 2-2. Variation in pizza delivery 2. By controlling variation, many fewer pizzas arrive early or late (dark shaded areas). Much higher "Sigma" score.

The first step in calculating sigma or in understanding its significance is to grasp what your customers expect. In the language of Six Sigma, customer requirements and expectations are called CTQs (critical to quality).

In the pizza example, one of the key customer requirements is timely delivery. Other requirements are likely to be related to the temperature of the pizza, the accuracy of the order, tastiness, and so on. In fact, one of the keys of Six Sigma is to better understand and assess how well a process performs on all CTQs, not just one or two.

We use the sigma measure to see how well or poorly a process performs and to give everyone a common way to express that measure. Table 2-1 summarizes the levels of sigma performance by how many defects would occur for every million opportunities or activities.

(Even if it would take a long time for your process to do a million items or tasks, don't worry; this scale is just a projection of the number that would happen if you did!)

SIX SIGMA AS A GOAL

Even if you're on the right track, you'll get run over if you just sit there.

—WILL ROGERS, HUMORIST

When a business violates important customer requirements, it is generating defects, complaints, and cost. The greater the number of defects that occur, the greater the cost of correcting them, as well as the risk of losing the customers. Ideally, your company wants to avoid any defects and the resulting cost in money and customer satisfaction.

But if you have lots of customers, some defects are bound to slip through, right? The problem is that even a seemingly low percentage of defects can mean a lot of unhappy customers. If your company processed 250,000 credit card bills a month and operated at 99.38 percent accuracy (4 sigma), you'd have about 1,550 unhappy customers every month. (How would you like to call them all and apologize?)

TABLE 2-1. Levels of Sigma Performance

Sigma Level	Defects per Million Opportunities
6	3.4
5	233
4	6,210
3	66,807
2	308,537
1	690,000

Remember, accuracy is just one requirement. If delivering the bills on time is another key factor and you're at the same level of performance (99.38 percent, or 4 sigma), you'd have yet another 1,550 defects (late bills) each month. So although 99.38 percent quality in credit bills sounds good, it's not so good for the customers (3,000 a month or more, in this case) who get hit with defects.

The goal of Six Sigma is to help people and processes aim high in aspiring to deliver defect-free products and services. The notion of zero defects is not at work here; Six Sigma recognizes that there's always some potential for defects, even in the best-run processes or best-built product. But at 99.9997 percent performance, Six Sigma sets a performance target where defects in many processes and products are almost nonexistent.

The impact of reaching Six Sigma can be easily seen when we compare performance in several aspects of our pizza business to a pretty good 99 percent (Table 2-2). As you can see, the costs of living with "only" 99 percent quality can have a significant impact on the bottom line.

The goal of Six Sigma is especially ambitious when you consider that prior to the start of a Six Sigma effort, many processes in many businesses operate at 1, 2, and 3 sigma levels, especially in intangible service and administrative areas. This means that from 66,000 to as many as 700,000 mistakes per million oppor-

TABLE 2-2. Performance Aspects for Pizza Business

ASPECT	WITH 99%	WITH SIX SIGMA
Orders lost/300,000 received	3,000	1
Complaints/50,000 pizzas baked	410	less than 2
Downtime/on-line ordering services	1.68 hours/week	1.8 seconds/week

tunities are being produced! Indeed, it's often a shock for people to see how poorly their processes and products perform.

A business might have been able to get away with such high defect rates in the past, but it's definitely not a formula for long-term success. Research suggests that when they experience the negative results of faulty products and processes, customers don't just sit around and feel depressed; they act. For example, here are some facts about the ripple effects of low-sigma performance:

- A dissatisfied customer will tell nine to ten people about an unhappy experience, even more people if the problem is not serious.
- The same customer will only tell five people if a problem is handled satisfactorily.
- Thirty-one percent of customers who experience service problems never register complaints, because it is "too much trouble," there is no easy channel of communication, or because they believe that no one cares.
- Of that 31 percent, as few as 9 percent will do additional business with the company.

In short, defects can lead to lost customers, and turned-off customers tell others about their experiences, making it that much more difficult to recover from defects. As customers get more and more demanding and impatient, these high levels of defects put a company in serious risk.

When taking up the Six Sigma banner, a business is saying, in effect: "We'd like to get as many of our customer-related activities and products performing as close to Six Sigma as we can." Because 3.4 defects per million is such a challenging goal, the more immediate objective may be to get from, say, 2 to 3 sigma. But that's not shabby either: It would mean reducing defects from more than 300,000 per million to fewer than 70,000.

Keeping customers happy is good and profitable for the business. A 5 percent increase in customer retention has been shown to increase profits more than 25 percent. It is estimated that companies lose 15 percent to 20 percent of revenues each year to ineffective, inefficient processes—although some might suggest that it's even higher. Six Sigma provides a goal that applies to both product and service activities and that sets attainable, short-term goals while striving for long-range business objectives.

SIX SIGMA AS A SYSTEM OF MANAGEMENT

A significant difference between Six Sigma and seemingly similar programs of past years is the degree to which management plays a key role in regularly monitoring program results and accomplishments. When Jack Welch introduced the Six Sigma program at GE, he told senior executives that 40 percent of their annual bonus would be based on their involvement and success in implementing Six Sigma.

That focused executive attention on turbocharging Six Sigma in their individual divisions. Training in GE was given a huge boost, and thousands of teams were trained in large sessions. At the same time, executives throughout GE participated in days and sometimes weeks of Six Sigma training.

But training alone is not a management system. A management system involves accountability for results and ongoing reviews to ensure results. With both accountability and regular reviews, managers can begin to use Six Sigma as a guide to leading their businesses.

The example of Starwood Hotels, which owns and operates such top hotel brands as Westin, Sheraton, and several luxury and resort hotels, shows how Six Sigma is being ingrained into management. At Starwood, which has launched the first Six Sigma program in the hospitality industry, managers at all levels are held accountable for a variety of measures:

* Customer satisfaction
* Key process performance
* Scorecard metrics on how the business is running
* Profit-and-loss statements
* Employee attitude

These measures provide feedback on the performance of the hotels and regions.

At regular meetings, managers review key measures within their hotels and select new Six Sigma projects that target those measures that have fallen off. If, say, guest complaints have risen, the hotel management will charter a Six Sigma team to find out why and to take corrective action. Moreover, good solutions developed at one hotel can be communicated and adopted as best practices, making service better for guests at other Starwood hotels. The net effect is to make Six Sigma a means of responding to critical business needs and ingraining proactive, customer-focused management into the daily routine.

As a management system, though, Six Sigma is not owned by senior leaders (although their role is critical) or driven by middle management (although their participation is key). The ideas, solutions, process discoveries, and improvements that arise from Six Sigma take place at the front lines of the organization. Six Sigma companies are striving to put more responsibility into the hands of the people who work directly with customers.

In short, Six Sigma is a system that combines both strong leadership and grassroots energy and involvement. In addition, the benefits of Six Sigma are not just financial. People at all levels of a Six Sigma company find that better understanding of customers, clearer processes, meaningful measures, and powerful improvement tools make their work more effective, less chaotic, and often more rewarding.

SUMMARY: SIX THEMES OF SIX SIGMA

We can distill the critical elements of Six Sigma into six themes. These principles—supported by the many Six Sigma tools and methods we'll be presenting throughout this book—will give you a preview of what Six Sigma will look like in your organization.

THEME ONE: GENUINE FOCUS ON THE CUSTOMER

As mentioned, companies launching Six Sigma have often been appalled to find how little they really understand about their customers.

In Six Sigma, customer focus becomes the top priority. For example, the measures of Six Sigma performance begin with the customer. Six Sigma improvements are defined by their impact on customer satisfaction and value.

THEME TWO: DATA- AND FACT-DRIVEN MANAGEMENT

Six Sigma takes the concept of "management by fact" to a new, more powerful level. Despite the attention paid in recent years to improved information systems, knowledge management, and so on, many business decisions are still being based on opinions and assumptions. Six Sigma discipline begins by clarifying what measures are key to gauging business performance and then gathers data and analyzes key variables. Then problems can be much more effectively defined, analyzed, and resolved—permanently.

At a more down-to-earth level, Six Sigma helps managers answer two essential questions to support data-driven decisions and solutions.

1. What data/information do I really need?
2. How do we use that data/information to maximum benefit?

THEME THREE: PROCESSES ARE WHERE THE ACTION IS

Whether focused on designing products and services, measuring performance, improving efficiency and customer satisfaction, or even running the business, Six Sigma positions the process as the key vehicle of success. One of the most remarkable breakthroughs in Six Sigma efforts to date has been convincing leaders and managers—particularly in service-based functions and industries—that mastering processes is a way to build competitive advantage in delivering value to customers.

THEME FOUR: PROACTIVE MANAGEMENT

Most simply, being proactive means acting in advance of events rather than reacting to them. In the real world, though, proactive management means making habits out of what are, too often, neglected business practices: defining ambitious goals and reviewing them frequently, setting clear priorities, focusing on problem prevention rather than firefighting, and questioning why we do things instead of blindly defending them.

Far from being boring or overly analytical, being truly proactive is a starting point for creativity and effective change. Six Sigma, as we'll see, encompasses tools and practices that replace reactive habits with a dynamic, responsive, proactive style of management.

THEME FIVE: BOUNDARYLESS COLLABORATION

"Boundarylessness" is one of Jack Welch's mantras for business success. Years before launching Six Sigma, GE's chairman was working to break down barriers and to improve teamwork up, down, and across organizational lines. The opportunities available through improved collaboration within companies and with vendors and customers are huge. Billions of dollars are lost every day because of disconnects and outright competition between groups that should be working for a common cause: providing value to customers.

THEME SIX: DRIVE FOR PERFECTION; TOLERATE FAILURE

How can you be driven to achieve perfection and yet also tolerate failure? In essence, though, the two ideas are complementary. No company will get even close to Six Sigma without launching new ideas and approaches—which always involve some risk. If people who see possible ways to be closer to perfect are too afraid of the consequences of mistakes, they'll never try.

Fortunately, the techniques we'll review for improving performance include a significant dose of risk management so the downside of setbacks or failures is limited. The bottom line, though, is that any company that makes Six Sigma its goal will have to keep pushing to be ever more perfect while being willing to accept—and manage—occasional setbacks.

WHERE YOU STAND

You may be saying to yourself, "We're already doing some of those things." But remember, we've already noted that much of Six Sigma is not new. What is new is its ability to bring together all these themes into a coherent management process.

Bear in mind that Six Sigma is a gradual process. It starts with a dream or a vision: the goal of near-perfect products and services and superb customer satisfaction. If you are willing to take on this challenge and if your company is willing to support your effort, you will find that few endeavors in your career yield as much satisfaction. In the next chapter, we talk about your role in Six Sigma and the kinds of action you can take to be a winner.

CHAPTER 3

SIX SIGMA IN YOUR ORGANIZATION

If your organization decides to implement Six Sigma, there's no telling precisely what that path will look like. "But," you may wonder, "if Six Sigma is about perfection and consistency, shouldn't there be one right way?" If there is, it hasn't been found yet. The truth is, organizations are different, and these differences justify varying approaches to implementing the Six Sigma change process.

IMPLEMENTING SIX SIGMA: THREE BASIC ON-RAMPS

Think of Six Sigma as a road to a new and better future for your organization. This highway has three possible "on-ramps," or approaches, each taking a different kind of route and perhaps taking you to a somewhat different destination. The route your organization chooses will determine the scope and depth of Six Sigma's impact on you and your colleagues.

ON-RAMP 1: THE BUSINESS TRANSFORMATION

Is your company getting behind in the market, losing money, failing to deliver on new products? Have new customers, acquisitions, or technologies created opportunities for a revitalized organization? Have people fallen into lazy habits and need a wake-up call? Are recent successes creating a flurry of activity that needs focus and foundation?

From our experience, observant employees and managers can often sense the need for a company to break away from old habits and to transform itself. For those organizations with the need, vision, and drive to launch Six Sigma as a full-scale change initiative, this first on-ramp, *business transformation*, is the right approach.

If you find yourself in the midst of a transformational Six Sigma implementation, it may feel as though senior managers are pounding out a new rhythm for the organization. Communication will be intensive and widespread: videos with top leaders and peers extolling the virtues of Six Sigma, brown-bag lunches and road shows explaining and discussing what Six Sigma is and how it will help, articles in the company newspaper, and explanations from department managers. You may start hearing such phrases as "a new company culture," "a way of life," or "the key to our future."

Dramatic change will be in the air. Everywhere, management will be trying to drive results from the changes and to control their impact. As an employee, you may find yourself on a Six Sigma team challenged to improve a critical business process or a key product.

Teams chartered along the business-transformation highway are often asked to look at key process areas and to make recommendations for change. These teams may scrutinize

- How the company distributes its products
- The effectiveness of the sales process
- New-product development
- Critical customer complaints
- Product defects and habitual problems
- Information systems critical to business decision making
- Large-scale cost reductions

If your company chooses the business-transformation on-ramp, you'll know it! This approach will have an impact on your work, how you measure your work, how you interact with customers and peers, and how you and your job performance are evaluated. Sooner or later, Six Sigma will become a 600-pound gorilla that can't be ignored.

Some of the companies that have adopted the business-transformation approach to Six Sigma are General Electric, Ford, Starwood Hotels, Bombardier, and 3M. People in these companies and others like them will tell you that it's a big effort.

ON-RAMP 2: STRATEGIC IMPROVEMENT

The middle on-ramp offers the most options. A *strategic-improvement* effort can be limited to one or two critical business needs, with teams and training aimed at addressing major opportunities or weaknesses. Or, it may be a Six Sigma effort concentrated in limited business units or functional areas of the organization.

In fact, to those directly involved, the strategic-improvement approach can seem as all-encompassing as the all-out corporatewide effort, but it simply is not as extensive or ambitious as the most aggressive efforts. On the other hand, a number of companies that have started with the more limited strategic focus have later expanded Six Sigma into a full-scale corporate change initiative, and yours may evolve that way, too.

Businesses that have taken the strategic-improvement on-ramp (from our observation and as of this writing) include Johnson & Johnson, Sears, American Express, and Sun Microsystems. A couple of examples of this approach follow.

- A large medical equipment and supplies company launched its Six Sigma effort to address key issues in manufacturing defects, costs, and productivity. For the manufacturing group, this very aggressive, engaging initiative continues, but few other parts of the business had any exposure to Six Sigma. Encouraged by the successes of that first manufacturing-based effort, the company has since launched a new effort to address critical warehousing and distribution problems. But so far, Six Sigma has not been adopted as a corporatewide theme for change.

- A leader in innovative computer systems and software embarked on a companywide Six Sigma effort in early

2000. Although the initiative has been described as a trans-formational effort, so far it has focused primarily on a few limited priorities. It's likely that this company's Six Sigma endeavor will become all encompassing, but to date, "the jury is still out."

ON-RAMP 3: PROBLEM SOLVING

The problem-solving on-ramp takes the most leisurely route to Six Sigma improvement. This approach targets nagging and persistent problems—often ones that have been the focus of earlier but unsuccessful improvement efforts—with people trained in the comprehensive Six Sigma tool set. These tools, as we'll see a bit later, lead to better problem analysis and solutions, based on facts and real understanding of causes and needs.

The problem-solving approach is best for companies that want to tap into the benefits of Six Sigma methods without creating major change ripples within the organization. If your business takes this approach, there's a strong probability that only a few people will be significantly engaged in the effort—unless, of course, it gets ramped up later. The benefit of this approach is in focusing on meaningful issues and addressing their root causes, using data and effective analysis rather than plain old gut feel.

As an example of this on-ramp, a major real estate company is running a few training classes and putting people to work on some key problems. Although the company will have a handful of Black Belts trained and some projects completed in a few months, that's about all you can predict for now. This company, like most others taking a problem-solving route, is really just kicking the tires on the Six Sigma vehicle.

WHICH ROUTE IS RIGHT?

You can probably guess that the depth of commitment, or on-ramp, chosen by your company will depend on what's best for that organization. Each on-ramp has some advantages and some risks. If you find yourself in a business-transformation initiative, you can look forward to rapid change and likely to some significant improvements within a few months. On the other hand, it's almost certain to be somewhat chaotic and certainly challenging to muster the people and time to meet the demands of this take-no-prisoners approach.

The strategic-improvement approach can help a company to focus on higher-priority opportunities and to limit the challenges of managing and selling change to your entire business. However, this on-ramp can create frustration by making some people feel left out of the process or uncertainty on how to align parts of the organization that are doing Six Sigma with those that are not.

The problem-solving approach is least disruptive and gives a company a chance to get a feel for how Six Sigma tools work. Unfortunately, this on-ramp is also deceptively risky. It doesn't fix underlying organizational problems or take a broad view of making change successful. It's like putting out fires without getting the tinder out of the basement.

As in many endeavors, what may be most important, no matter which level of effort your company launches, is to do it well. You and your colleagues will have to understand and play some new roles that support the Six Sigma system.

NEW ROLES FOR MANAGERS AND EMPLOYEES

Once management has chosen an on-ramp to Six Sigma, the real work is up to a collection of business leaders, team members, team leaders, and facilitators. Some people's roles may have martial arts names: Black Belt, Green Belt, and Master Black Belt. (Reportedly, these titles were coined by a Motorola improvement expert with a passion for karate.) Other roles will have more familiar titles.

Black Belt

All things considered, this is probably the most critical new role in Six Sigma. The Black Belt is the full-time person dedicated to tackling critical change opportunities and driving them to achieve results. The Black Belt leads, inspires, manages, delegates, coaches, and "baby-sits" colleagues and becomes almost expert in tools for assessing problems and fixing or designing processes and products.

Usually, the Black Belt works alongside a team assigned to a specific Six Sigma project. He or she is primarily responsible for getting the team started, building their confidence, observing and participating in training, managing team dynamics, and keeping the project moving to successful results.

Without a strong and tireless Black Belt, Six Sigma teams are usually not effective. The Black Belt must possess many skills, including strong problem solving, the ability to collect and analyze data, organizational savvy, leadership and coaching experience, and good administrative sense. Moreover, he or she must be adept at project management—the art and science of getting things done on time through the efforts of others.

Black Belts—many of whom are drawn from the ranks of middle management or are high future managers—typically serve a term of eighteen months to two years, completing four to eight projects and/or handling special assignments. Most companies view Black Belt–hood as a springboard to other opportunities, including promotions and bonuses. Quite a few Black Belts find that they love the type of work the job entails and take up a new career as full-time Six Sigma persons.

MASTER BLACK BELT

In most organizations, the Master Black Belt (MBB, pronounced em-bee-bee) serves as a coach and mentor or consultant to Black Belts working on a variety of projects. In most instances, the MBB is a real expert in Six Sigma analytical tools, often with a background in engineering or science or an advanced degree in business.

In some companies, the MBB plays more of an organizational change agent role, helping promote use of Six Sigma methods and solutions. The MBB may also become a part-time Six Sigma trainer for Black Belts and other groups. Finally, the MBB may get involved in special Six Sigma–related projects: for example, investigating customer requirements or developing measures for key processes.

Some Master Black Belts got their basic experience in the "quality" departments of their organizations. More and more, however, you'll find that after serving a tour of duty as a Black Belt, they found their calling and decided to stay involved in business improvement. Of course, they have to have the right skills to fill the role of an MBB in their organizations.

As a coach, the MBB's job is to ensure that the Black Belt and his/her team stay on track, complete their work properly, and pass "tollgates"—key tasks for each step of the Six Sigma improvement process. Often, too, the Master Black Belt provides advice and even hands-on help for such tasks as collecting data, doing statistical analyses, designing experiments, and communicating with key managers.

Like most coaches, the MBB will have several Black Belts under his or her care. In most of our client companies, the MBBs themselves form a "team," or at least a network, advising one another and working to identify opportunities and challenges in the Six Sigma effort.

Black Belts are more numerous and are fundamental to most Six Sigma efforts. Master Black Belts pay a critical role in sustaining the momentum of change, cost savings, and improved customer experience.

GREEN BELT

A Green Belt is someone trained in Six Sigma skills, often to the same level as a Black Belt. But the Green Belt still has a "real" job and serves as either a team member or a part-time Six Sigma team leader. Some companies, most notably GE, have required large segments of their population to be trained as Green Belts. The role of the Green Belt is to bring the new concepts and tools of Six Sigma right to the day-to-day activities of the business.

CHAMPION AND/OR SPONSOR

These titles are common to Six Sigma efforts. Usually, a Champion is an executive or a key manager who initiates and supports (sponsors) a Black Belt or a team project.

Having a Champion or a Sponsor is very important. This role sends a critical message: The Champion, a fairly senior person, is ultimately accountable. In other words, Six Sigma results are not delegated down many layers in the business but remain in the hands of senior and key middle management.

The Champion or Sponsor is often a member of the *Leadership Council,* or steering committee, for the business. Sometimes, a Sponsor will oversee one or more Champions. In any case, the responsibilities of the Champion are to

- Ensure that projects stay aligned with overall business goals and provide direction when they don't
- Keep other members of the leadership team informed on the progress of projects
- Provide or cajole needed resources, such as time, money, and help from others, for the team
- Conduct the tollgate reviews
- Negotiate conflicts, overlaps, and linkages with other Six Sigma projects

Unfortunately, the Champion/Sponsor role tends to get the least training and preparation, so it can be one of the weakest links in Six Sigma efforts, especially early on.

IMPLEMENTATION LEADER

This role may go by other names: Vice President of Six Sigma, Chief Sigma Officer, Grand Poobah. This individual orchestrates the entire Six Sigma effort. He or she is often at the corporate vice president level, reporting directly to the CEO, president, or another top executive.

The Implementation Leader is either a seasoned professional in organizational improvement or quality or a respected inside executive with significant company experience and strong leadership and administrative abilities. This is a high-stress, high-demand job with short-term goals, long-term visions, and significant accountability.

Like the Black Belt, the Implementation Leader is often a temporary position, with the leader moving on to another executive or management position after a few years. The ultimate goal of the Implementation Leader is to drive Six Sigma thinking, tools, and habits across the organization and to help the effort reap financial and customer benefits.

In many ways, the Implementation Leader serves as the conscience of the top-management team, helping its members keep Six Sigma practices and priorities high on their agenda. He or she will also be primarily responsible for executing implementation plans.

CONSEQUENCES OF NEW ROLES

Because they are the most specialized and technical of the Six Sigma roles, the Black Belt and the Master Black Belt are often subject to certification, usually based on passing a test and completing a certain number of projects. There is no formal or official guideline for certification, though, so the criteria are not consistent. In some companies, certification is a big deal; in others, more emphasis is put on results.

Taking on a new Six Sigma role can be both exciting and scary for many people, even though very few we've met through the years have regretted taking on these new and sometimes unfamiliar responsibilities. Most people admit that the work was challenging and required a lot of energy and effort.

If you find yourself being considered for a Six Sigma role, you may want to ask yourself and/or the others in the organization the following questions.

- If it's a full-time job, how long will the assignment last, and what happens after I complete the Six Sigma assignment?
- Who will be my boss during the assignment?
- How will my work be measured, and how will I be rewarded?
- If it's a part-time job, will time be freed up to work on Six Sigma responsibilities?
- What kind of testing or certification process will I need to pass? By when?

- How will the organization really look on my work in the team? Will it seem as important as my "regular" job?

The answers to these and other questions will vary with the specific implementation decisions in your organization. As we've noted, the ability to adapt Six Sigma to fit the needs of various kinds of businesses is one of the reasons it is proving so effective in promoting change and dollar benefits in so many companies.

CHAPTER 4

THE SIX SIGMA TEAM'S PROBLEM-SOLVING PROCESS

DMAIC

A re you having fun with Six Sigma's alphabet soup so far? We've seen "CTQs" and "MBBs" and now we're going to look at perhaps the most important string of letters: DMAIC.

Improvement, problem-solving, and process-design teams are the most visible and active component of a Six Sigma effort, especially at first. These teams, as we've noted, are created to solve organizational problems and to capitalize on opportunities. Led by a Black Belt or a Green Belt, the teams usually number three to ten members (five or six is best) representing different parts of the process being worked on.

One of the cool things about Six Sigma teams is their diversity: Members frequently come from different departments, job levels, backgrounds, skills, and seniority. On the team, everyone is, by and large, an equal, and the contributions of each member are key to achieving the breakthroughs sought in a Six Sigma effort.

In bringing a diverse team together, it's critical to have a common process, or model, that all members can share to get their work done. The answer to this need in Six Sigma is the DMAIC (pronounced duh-MAY-ick) process: Define, Measure, Analyze, Improve, and Control. By following this process, a flexible but powerful set of five steps for making improvements happen and stick, the team works from a statement of the problem to implementation of a solution, with lots of activities in between. In working through this DMAIC process, the team is also interacting with the larger organization, interviewing customers, gathering data, and talking to people whose work will be affected by the team's solution recommendations.

Of course, Six Sigma teams, or DMAIC teams, don't just spring into existence. Just as important are the steps that go into choosing the projects, forming the team, and shifting the team's work into the real world. In this chapter, we'll look first at the steps of forming and disbanding a DMAIC team. We'll also look at the steps and tools of the DMAIC problem-solving model.

THE DMAIC TEAM LIFE CYCLE

Several broad phases apply to the life cycle of almost all DMAIC teams, although these phases will vary from company to company.

PHASE 1: IDENTIFYING AND SELECTING THE PROJECT(S)

In this phase, management reviews a list of potential Six Sigma projects and selects the most promising to be tackled by a team. Setting good priorities is difficult but very important to making the team's work pay off.

We counsel leaders to pick projects based on the "two Ms": *meaningful* and *manageable*. A project has to have real benefit to the business and customers and has to be small enough so the team can get it done. At the end of this phase, your leadership group should have identified high-priority problems and given them some preliminary boundaries.

The group's challenge is to clearly articulate the business necessity of the project. For example, How much is the problem costing the company? or How much of an opportunity will the improvement provide? Usually, a Champion or a Sponsor is selected for each project as well.

PHASE 2: FORMING THE TEAM

Hand-in-hand with problem recognition comes team and team leader (Black Belt or Green Belt) selection. Naturally, the two efforts are related. Management will try to select team members who have good working knowledge of the situation but who are not so deeply rooted in it that they may be part of the problem.

Smart leaders realize that DMAIC team participation should not be handed to idle slackers. If you are chosen for a team, it means that you are viewed as someone with the smarts and the energy to be a real contributor!

PHASE 3: DEVELOPING THE CHARTER

The Charter is a key document that provides a written guide to the problem or project. The Charter includes the reason for pursuing the project, the goal, a basic project plan, scope and other considerations, and a review of roles and responsibilities. Typically, parts of the Charter are drafted by the Champion and added to and refined by the team. In fact, the Charter usually changes over the course of the DMAIC project.

PHASE 4: TRAINING THE TEAM

Training is a high priority in Six Sigma. In fact, some people say that "training" is a misnomer because a lot of "classroom" time is spent doing real work on the Black Belt's or team's project.

The focus of the training is on the DMAIC process and tools. Typically, this training lasts one to four weeks. The time is spread out, though. After the first week, the team leader and/or team members go back to their regular work but budget a key portion of their time to working on the project. After a two- to five-week "intersession" comes the second training session, then another work period and another week of training.

PHASE 5: DOING DMAIC AND IMPLEMENTING SOLUTIONS

Nearly all DMAIC teams are responsible for implementing their own solutions, not just handing them off to another group.

Teams must develop project plans, training, pilots, and procedures for their solutions and are responsible for both putting them in place and ensuring that they work—by measuring and monitoring results—for a meaningful period of time.

PHASE 6: HANDING OFF THE SOLUTION

Eventually, of course, the DMAIC team will disband, and members return to their "regular" jobs or move on to the next project. Because they frequently work in the areas affected by their solutions, team members often go forward to help manage the new process or solution and ensure its success.

The hand-off is sometimes marked by a formal ceremony in which the official owner, often called "Process Owner," of the solutions accepts responsibility to sustain the gains achieved by the team. (Dancing and fun may go on until the wee hours of the morning. . . .) Just as important, the DMAIC team members take a new set of skills and experience to apply to issues that arise every day.

THE DMAIC PROBLEM-SOLVING MODEL

"What," you may ask, "makes DMAIC different from or better than other problem-solving techniques?" (If so, you're already practicing one of the key skills of Six Sigma management: asking good questions!)

DMAIC as just a set of letters or steps is not better. But what is better is what you do as you move through the five DMAIC steps. The biggest differences or advantages of DMAIC probably boil down to these seven items:

1. *Measuring the problem.* In DMAIC, you don't just assume that you understand what the problem is; you have to prove (validate) it with facts.
2. *Focusing on the customer.* The external customer is always important, even if you're just trying to cut costs in a process.

3. *Verifying root cause.* In the bad old days, if a team agreed on a cause, that was proof enough. In the good new days (a Six Sigma world), you've got to prove your cause with, again, facts and data.

4. *Breaking old habits.* Solutions coming out of DMAIC projects should not just be minor changes in crusty old processes. Real change and results take creative new solutions.

5. *Managing risks.* Testing and perfecting solutions—working out the "bugs"—is an essential part of Six Sigma discipline and pretty good common sense.

6. *Measuring results.* As we've noted, the follow-up to any solution is to verify its real impact: more reliance on facts.

7. *Sustaining change.* Even the best of new "best practices" developed by a DMAIC team can die quickly if not nurtured and supported. Making change last is the final key to this more enlightened problem-solving approach.

There's more to DMAIC than these seven advantages, but they're surely the most important. As we review the five DMAIC steps, you'll get a better idea how the process works.

STEP 1: *DEFINE* THE PROBLEM

The first step sets the stage for the project as a whole and often poses the greatest challenge to a team. The team must grapple with an array of questions: What are we working on? Why are we working on this particular problem? Who is the customer? What are the customer's requirements? How is the work currently being done? What are the benefits of making the improvement?

These kinds of questions, fundamental business thinking, drive new and original ways of thinking about business problems that in the past were too often ignored. Once these questions are answered—at least in a draft form—the DMAIC Charter can be developed.

Charters vary from company to company but typically include

- *A business case:* Why is this particular opportunity being chosen?
- *Problem/opportunity and goal statements:* What's the specific problem or pain being addressed, and what results will be sought?
- *Constraints/assumptions:* What limitations are placed on the project or resource expectations being made?
- *Scope:* How much of the process and/or range of issues is "in bounds"?
- *Players and roles:* Who are the team members, Champion, and other stakeholders?
- *Preliminary plan:* When will each phase (D, M, A, I, and C) be completed?

This project blueprint is intended to define and narrow the project's focus, clarify the results being sought, confirm value to the business, establish boundaries and resources for the team, and help the team communicate its goals and plans. The project blueprint is the first, and often most important, tollgate that must be signed off on by the project Champion before the team proceeds.

The team's next job is to identify the most important player in any process: the customer. Customers may be either internal (within the business) or external (paying customers). It's the job of the Black Belt and the team to get a good fix on what customers want—especially the external customers, whose "purchase decisions" determine whether the company continues to make money, grow, and so on.

This work, involving the voice of the customer (VOC) can be challenging. Customers themselves are often not sure about what they want or have trouble expressing it. They are generally pretty good, though, about describing what they don't want. So the team must listen to the "voice of the customer" and translate the customer's language into meaningful requirements, as illustrated in Table 4-1.

TABLE 4-1. Translating the VOC into Requirements

CUSTOMER SAYS	MEANING TO OUR BUSINESS	CUSTOMER REQUIREMENT
"Your deliveries take too long."	We are seen as slow in making promised deliveries.	Orders must be delivered within three working days of receipt of purchase order.
"I didn't know I had to bring this thing back within seven days in order to get a refund."	We are unclear or too strict in our returns policy.	Clear communication of returns policies is essential.

Next, we create a high-level diagram of the process the team will be working on. The notion of high level is critical: At this point, you do not want to bury the team in a large, bewildering, spaghettilike map of a detailed process flow. So this first diagram usually shows about five to ten major steps describing the current, or as-is process. This enables everyone on the team to have the same picture of the process and to work from the same assumptions. Creating the diagram also sets the stage for the next major step—Measure—by giving the team an idea of where it may want to collect data. (To learn about the technique used for these diagrams, see Chapter 6.)

STEP 2: *MEASURE*

Measure is a logical follow-up to Define and is a bridge to the next step: Analyze. The Measure step has two main objectives:

1. Gather data to validate and to quantify the problem/opportunity. Usually, this is critical information to refine and complete the first full project Charter.

2. Begin teasing out facts and numbers that offer clues about the causes of the problem.

Remember, Six Sigma teams take a process view of the business and use that view to set priorities and to make good decisions about what measures are needed. As shown in Figure 4-1, a process has three main categories of measures:

1. *Output or Outcome:* the end results of the process. Output measures focus on immediate results (deliveries, defects, complaints) and outcomes on longer terms impacts (profit, satisfaction, etc.)
2. *Process:* things that can be tracked and measured. These items usually help the team start to pinpoint causes of the problem.
3. *Input:* things coming into the process for change into outputs. Of course, bad inputs can create bad outputs, so input measures also help identify possible causes of a problem.

The DMAIC team's first priority is almost always the output measures that best quantify the current problems. This baseline measure is the data used to complete the Charter; sometimes, if the problem turns out to be smaller than or different from expectations, the project may be canceled or revamped.

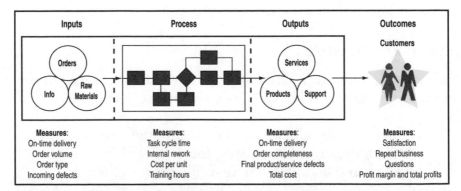

FIGURE 4-1. Types and Examples of Measures. There are many ways to measure performance at each phase: Input, Process and Output. "Outcome" measures look at long-term impact and results.

A BIT MORE DETAIL: OUTPUT *Y*S AND PROCESS *X*S

In Six Sigma talk, two letters (*Y* and *X*) are used to represent the three kinds of measures. After a while, you'll get used to taking in these terms.

Y stands for measures of the *results* and *outcomes* of a process. In other words, *Y* is pretty much the same as an output measure. *Y* can also come to represent a goal or objectives, as in: "Our big *Y* is to reduce cycle time to one day." The *Y* measure is cycle time.

Y measures often link to customer requirements. Other *Y* measures—profit margin, for example—may be important to you or your business but not so much to your customer.

X stands for measures that come from the process or the inputs. A business process usually has many possible *X* measures, such as number of staff or cost of raw materials or length of a phone call. The challenge for the DMAIC team is to figure out which of these *X*s has the most impact on the problem being tackled. When the team finds it, that *X* is the "root cause."

The link or relationship between the input and process activities and the results, or outputs, is sometimes represented as an equation:

$$Y = f(Xs)$$

This means that the results (*Y*s) you get are a function of (*f*)—the stuff that comes before (the *X*s). Companies that can figure out how this equation really works have a big advantage in knowing how to improve customer satisfaction, profits, speed, and so forth. In Six Sigma, reaching that level of knowledge is a "big *Y*."

Process and a select few input measures are targeted to begin getting data on potential causes. Once it has determined what to measure, the DMAIC team forms a "data collection plan." This is often where team members move from the comfortable sequestered conference or training room into the real world of getting people to help count and quantify what's going on in the business.

Some of the most important techniques learned in good DMAIC training involve how to collect data, how many to count (sampling), and how often to count it. Getting cooperation from customers, colleagues, and suppliers, is usually critical. In fact, many people's first exposure to Six Sigma projects is being asked to help collect data.

(*Note:* Some Black Belts or teams are lucky and find that the data they need is already available in computer systems or file cabinets. These teams get to skip data collection. But usually, some kind of new data is needed during the course of the project.)

A common milestone in the Measure step is to develop an initial "sigma measure" for the process being fixed. (In some companies, it's mandatory; others make it optional.) As noted in Chapter 2, the sigma measure is good at helping compare performance of very different processes and relating them to customer requirements. With an early read on the number or count of defects or unwanted outputs of a process, an early sigma can be calculated.

STEP 3: *ANALYZE*

In this step, the DMAIC team delves into the details, enhances its understanding of the process and problem, and, if all goes as intended, identifies the culprit behind the problem. The team uses the Analyze step to find the "root cause."

Sometimes, the root causes of a problem are evident. When they are, teams can move through analysis quickly. Often, though, root causes are buried under piles of paperwork and old processes, lost among the complexities of many people doing work in their own way and not documenting it, year after year. When this happens, the team can spend several weeks or months applying an array of tools and testing various ideas before finally closing the case.

One of the principles of good DMAIC problem solving is to consider many types of causes, so as not to let biases or past experience cloud the team's judgment. Some of the common cause categories to be explored are

• *Methods:* the procedures or techniques used in doing the work

A BIT MORE DETAIL: CALCULATING SIGMA

Figuring the sigma for most processes is pretty easy. A calculator is helpful, but no advanced math is needed. What is needed is basic data and definitions for the following:

- The "unit," or item being delivered to the customer

- The "requirements" that make the unit good or bad for the customer

- The number of requirements, or defect opportunities, for each unit

For example, in the pizza business, our unit is a pizza! We determine the four main "requirements": correct ingredients, hot, on time, and undamaged. These four requirements are also the four "defect opportunities" for each pizza.

We collect data on 500 delivered pizzas and find that 25 were late, 10 were too cold, 7 were damaged, and 16 had wrong ingredients. To calculate sigma, we take the total number of defects counted, divide by the total number of units, and multiply by the number of defect opportunities:

$$\frac{(25 + 10 + 7 + 16)}{500 \times 4}$$

This gives us 58 ÷ 2000, or 0.029; we call this defects per opportunity (DPO).

As we explained in Chapter 2, we usually consider 1 million opportunities, so that would be 29,000 defects per million opportunities (DPMO). Now all you do is look up that DPMO number in a table to find what sigma it represents. (You can find the table in the Appendix, page 87.) In this case, the pizza process is performing at about 3.3 sigma.

- *Machines:* the technology, such as computers, copiers, or manufacturing equipment, used in a work process

- *Materials:* the data, instructions, numbers or facts, forms, and files that, if flawed, will have a negative impact on the output

- *Measures:* faulty data resulting from measuring a process or changing people's actions on the basis of what's measured and how

- *Mother Nature:* environmental elements, from weather to economic conditions, that impact how a process or a business performs
- *People:* a key variable in how all these these other elements combine to produce business results

(These cause categories are sometimes dubbed the "5Ms and 1P.")

DMAIC teams narrow their search for causes by what we call the *Analyze cycle.* The cycle begins by combining experience, data/measures, and a review of the process and then forming an initial guess, or hypothesis of the cause. The team then looks for more data and other evidence to see whether it fits with the suspected cause. The cycle of analysis continues, with the hypothesis being refined or rejected until the true root cause is identified and verified with data.

One of the big challenges in the Analyze step is to use the right tools. With luck, fairly simple tools can get to the cause. When causes go deeper or when the relationship between the problem and other factors is complex and hidden, more advanced statistical techniques may be required to identify and to verify the cause.

STEP 4: *IMPROVE*

This step—solution and action—is where many people are tempted to jump right from the start of the project. (We've heard folks say, "It's how we've been conditioned: 'See problem. Kill problem.'")

In fact, the habit of starting to solve a problem without first understanding it is so strong that many teams find it a challenge to stick with the objective rigor of the DMAIC process. When they see the value of asking questions, checking assumptions, and using data, though, team members realize how much better this Six Sigma approach is.

Before even beginning to develop solutions, many teams go back to their Charters and modify their problem and goal statements to reflect their discoveries to this point. It's common to reaffirm the value of the project with the DMAIC team Champions. Teams may also modify the scope of their project, based on a better understanding of the problem and the process. But once the team has realigned its goals, Improve is the step for finally planning and achieving results.

Surprisingly, this may be easier said than done. Truly creative solutions that address the underlying causes of the problem and that people working in the process find acceptable don't grow on trees. And once new ideas are developed, they have to be tested, refined, and implemented

Why are truly new solutions at such a premium? One reason may be that the team has been used to current approaches (and engaged in measurement and analysis) for so long that kicking free of old thinking is difficult. The other reason is that truly creative solutions are always rare events.

Assumption busting and other creativity exercises help the team shake up its thinking and approach idea generation in new ways. The team may also look at other companies or other groups in their business to see whether they can borrow "best practices" from elsewhere.

Once several potential solutions have been proposed, the analytical headsets go back on, and several criteria, including costs and likely benefits, are used to select the most promising and practical solutions. The "final" solution or series of changes must always be approved by the Champion and often by the entire leadership team.

At this point, Improve becomes Implement. (In fact, some companies add a second I and call the process DMAIIC.)

Implementation is not a "just do it" activity. DMAIC solutions have to be carefully managed and tested. Small-scale pilots are practically mandatory; teams go through careful "potential problem analysis" to determine what could go wrong and prepare to prevent or manage difficulties. New changes have to be "sold" to organization members whose participation is critical. Data must be gathered to track and to verify the impact (and unintended consequences) of the solution.

Sound like a lot of work? Well, it usually is. But DMAIC teams have found that it's also a thrill to see their efforts begin to pay off as defects are reduced, costs eliminated, and customers better served.

STEP 5: *CONTROL*

One of our colleagues often describes organizations and processes as being like rubber bands. You can work hard to stretch them into all kinds of new and interesting shapes, but as soon as you let go, snap! It's back to its old shape.

Avoiding the "snap" back to old habits and processes is the main objective of the Control step. Ultimately, having a long-term impact on the way people work and ensuring that it lasts is as much about persuading and selling ideas as it is about measuring and monitoring results. Both are essential.

Specific Control tasks that DMAIC Black Belts and teams much complete include:

- Developing a monitoring process to keep track of the changes they have set out
- Creating a response plan for dealing with problems that may arise
- Helping focus management's attention on a few critical measures that give them current information on the outcomes of the project (the Y) and key process measures, too (the Xs)

From the people standpoint, the team must

- "Sell" the project through presentations and demonstrations
- Hand off project responsibilities to those who do the day-to-day work
- Ensure support from management for the long-term goals of the project

It may be difficult to imagine walking away from a project that a team may have spent months on and going on to other projects or back to the "regular" job, but teams do it all the time. The ultimate success of the Six Sigma project rests with those who do the work in the area the project was focused on. Ideally, as these people see the value of the new solutions developed through the DMAIC process—and the results they offer—they too will begin to understand the potential that the Six Sigma system can provide.

SUMMARY

The DMAIC problem-solving process and the phases of the project cycle work hand-in-hand. DMAIC has often been referred to as iterative. This means that the line from Define to Control is not straight but rather jogs back and forth, revisiting earlier assumptions and filling places passed over in haste.

In a sense, the only thing that remains inviolate during a Six Sigma project is the need to be flexible in dealing with continuous change, the ability to absorb and to interpret information, and the need to remain open and attentive to the input of many stakeholders within and outside the immediate team. A team that can accomplish these things has few limits to its potential for solving problems and improving business performance.

CHAPTER 5

SURVIVOR'S GUIDE TO SIX SIGMA

A fundamental principle of Six Sigma is that the people close to the work are often best equipped to improve it. At the same time, organizational leaders need to provide direction and be fully engaged in the drive to build a better organization. In fact, one of the neat—if not always easy—tricks of Six Sigma is to create a process that is both top-down and bottom-up.

In this chapter, we review in more detail some of the likely impacts Six Sigma efforts may impose on you as an employee and some of the opportunities and challenges you should consider. (If you have questions about any of the role titles we mention, flip back to Chapter 3 for a quick review.)

COPING WITH THE CHANGE THAT SIX SIGMA BRINGS

If you are being sucked into the whirlwind of any organizational change, the experience can be inspiring but also, sometimes, threatening. Even when business leaders make a conscientious effort to communicate their plans and rationale for Six Sigma, a lot of questions will remain unanswered. These unanswered questions are usually not an attempt to keep people in the dark (despite what you might suspect) but instead arise from two understandable facts.

1. Leaders can't anticipate—let alone respond to—all the personal questions that arise when people wonder, "How will this affect me?"

2. Putting Six Sigma in place is not a step-by-step rote effort but rather an evolving learning experience. So usually, leaders don't have the answers to a lot of questions right away. If leaders do, those answers often change over time.

However, certain aspects of Six Sigma tend to happen in every organization, and we can give you some tips on what to anticipate and how to respond. Consider this chapter your guide to winning the *Survivor* game, in which you find yourself stranded on "Six Sigma Island."

CHALLENGE 1: BEING ASKED TO JOIN A SIX SIGMA TEAM

What this Means.   This should be good news. Six Sigma Black Belts and project Champions know that to throw just anybody on a team is a bad idea, so they look for people who have talent and knowledge: in other words, something to contribute.

How to Succeed.   Often, the call to join a DMAIC team is one of those offers you can't refuse. If you do have a choice, it's good to ask yourself, "Am I comfortable working in a team setting? Will my workload allow me the time to do a good job? Do I really have something to contribute? Will I have a say in what the team recommends or just be a pair of hands?"

In general, if a team is going to work on a project near and dear to your job, having input into the team's recommendations seems like enlightened self-interest. Ask yourself, " Do I want to be part of the problem or part of the solution?" In most cases, the answer will be obvious.

Assuming that you move forward into the new world of DMAIC team membership, you can still be on the alert for key success factors and do your part to ensure that they are in place. Some of the most important success factors are

* *An engaged Champion.* Does the team have a senior management sponsor who is interested in the outcome and who is willing to provide resources and support to the team?

- *Available time.* DMAIC team members can usually expect that their project will increase their workloads, but if none of your current responsibilities is lightened, the project may grind to a halt.

- *Influence or control.* Beware of your team's being asked (or deciding) to try to fix someone else's problem or process. Your team should include members responsible for or who participate in the part of the business you intend to change.

- *Alignment with other efforts.* Leaders sometimes forget or are unaware of similar or competing projects addressing the problem you're assigned to solve. Failure to iron out these overlaps or conflicts can cause big delays and disappointments. So if you see a misalignment, you should speak up!

- *Accountability.* Change rarely takes root unless people feel responsible for making it happen. You and your teammates should feel accountable for getting your projects done, as should the Champion and even your own boss, who may drag you away from the DMAIC work if he or she doesn't see it as important.

These are just some of the most important things to consider. The best way to survive and to thrive as a Six Sigma team member is to maintain a positive attitude, voice your views and respect those of others, and recognize the great opportunity you've been given to make meaningful change in your business.

CHALLENGE 2: ATTENDING SIX SIGMA TRAINING

What this Means.   Six Sigma training can be pretty extensive: from five days to four weeks. Fortunately, there are breaks between the weeks, and the training typically involves a lot of hands-on work on your projects. (Some teams make their fastest progress during the training itself.) Also, the skills and tools you gain are great for helping you contribute more to the business every day, not just while on a DMAIC team. (A lot of the training is about learning to ask better questions and get better answers!)

How to Succeed.   Go with an attitude open to learning. If you've had quality training or been involved in process improvement projects, you may feel that this will be repetitious, redundant, or the same old stuff again. But after the training starts, you'll almost certainly find that there's a lot to learn and many nuances that go into making Six Sigma projects successful.

Those of us who've been working professionally in Six Sigma or related areas for many years are amazed at how much we continue to learn all the time. However, those people who expect the training to be a waste of time will usually get the least out of the experience, although even they eventually realize how valuable it is!

The opportunity to work on a real project on your own or with a team means that the experience is usually much richer than routine classroom training. You'll gain from the perspectives of other people. At times, you may find that the other folks on your team or in your workshop are a challenge to work with, but that's just part of the process of making effective change happen.

A couple of special challenges of DMAIC training bear mentioning:

- *Short lead times.* Once companies decide to adopt a Six Sigma effort, they are often in a hurry to move forward. People may be told on Thursday that they are needed in a training class in another state on Monday. If that happens to you, try not to let it turn you off Six Sigma or cause you to miss out on the value the training itself can offer.

- *Mastering the statistics.* The depth of statistical content in Six Sigma Black Belt and Green Belt training can vary a lot. To some people, you can't do Six Sigma without a thorough knowledge of stats, but for most people, the priority is on the ability to use facts and to apply statistics when and where needed. If you need to learn a lot of statistics in a hurry, just remember that most companies offer help and coaching through Master Black Belts and other resources. Also, you can review basic statistics, practice using statistical software, or organize spreadsheets to help smooth out the road for you. Most people who start with a statistics phobia end up being very comfortable and competent with numbers.

By and large, even though it's a lot of work and very challenging, most people find that they enjoy their Six Sigma training and regard it as a valuable contributor to their development.

CHALLENGE 3: FINDING A DMAIC TEAM WORKING ON YOUR PROCESS

What this Means.   No, it's not like hearing that a *60 Minutes* crew is asking you for an investigative interview. It's usually a positive sign that needed improvements are in store for your area or process. With DMAIC, the focus will be on why problems exist, not on who is making them. ("Blame the process, not the people" is the mantra.) Also, a savvy Black Belt will be quite concerned about keeping you (a "stakeholder") positive and in gaining your support for any change efforts. The DMAIC team is not likely to try to push unworkable solutions down your throat.

How to Succeed.   First, realize that the Six Sigma team is not your enemy. If your work processes are important enough for management to charter a team, they are important enough to improve. You may have insights into the processes that the Black Belt or team doesn't. You can, in short, be valuable to the team. Also consider that change will happen with or without you. Getting on board early increases your chances of having a seat at the table later on. Finally, consider that the team is trying to make your work more meaningful, more impactful, more customer friendly, and more vital to the company. What would be better job security if it succeeds?

CHALLENGE 4: BEING ASKED TO GATHER DATA

What this Means.   After learning that a DMAIC project is focusing on issues in your area, you're likely to be asked to help get some data. Computers and the information technology group often don't offer the type of numbers or detail needed for DMAIC analysis. So Black Belts and their colleagues have to pull data from the process manually, using people in the process to count or to measure things. Yes, it may indeed mean some extra work for you. But again, though, it does not mean that you, your department, or anyone is being targeted for blame.

How to Succeed.   Measurement is not meant to be intentionally difficult though it can be a challenge. On the contrary, DMAIC teams are encouraged to make collecting data as simple and easy for you as possible. In return, you'll make their work more effective if you

- *Record data accurately.* Fudging the numbers won't help anyone figure out how to fix a problem. Be honest and precise.
- *Collect data consistently.* Cooperate and keep good records every day.
- *Ask questions.* If you don't understand what data you're being asked to gather, why it's needed, or how you're supposed to do it, speak up. Doing it wrong because you were confused will likely mean having to collect data all over again.
- *Offer suggestions.* If you think you can make the data gathering easier, let the Black Belt or team know.

CHALLENGE 5: BEING ASKED TO HELP IMPLEMENT A PROCESS SOLUTION

What this Means.   Well, there are going to be some changes, and you can either help make them work or get in the way. Guess which we'd prefer?

How to Succeed.   Being defensive will only put you in a bad light and cause the team to see you as uncooperative. Instead, approach the plan objectively; ask questions and offer constructive comments. Look for holes in the plan but also ways to stitch them up. Volunteer to help out. Better yet, you may want to volunteer yourself or your work area to help pilot a solution. That way, you'll get the training and experience first and be looked on as a pioneer—a leader and not just a survivor of Six Sigma!

IMPROVING YOUR JOB SKILLS THROUGH SIX SIGMA

So far, we've referred to all the wonderful benefits of Six Sigma without directly addressing the question of what's in it for you. Not that you couldn't be trusted to do your best with any Six Sigma challenge to come your way, but it's always nice to have a little self-interest in the challenge.

Six Sigma can give you not only challenges but also some nice benefits. These include what we call the "three Es."

EXPERIENCE

Whether as a team member, a Black Belt, or an employee of a key process, you will learn an important and powerful set of tools to improve and/or redesign work. You will master the DMAIC process—which has become a new industry standard for problem solving—and you will be able to show concrete results stemming from your project.

When you talk about the Six Sigma projects you have been involved in, you can say, "We accomplished this." "We saved this much money." "We reduced cycle time by 50 percent." "We increased customer satisfaction numbers by 25 percent." "We delivered more than $500,000 net income through quicker order fulfillment."

The ability to get things done and the numbers to document your accomplishments represent the holy grail of business aspirations. Whatever your background and technical experience—technology, operations, sales, human resources—Six Sigma experience will provide you with an overall business management perspective invaluable in the rest of your career.

EXPOSURE

Dollar for dollar, pound for pound, there are few better or quicker ways to get exposure in an organization than by participating in an important Six Sigma project. In fact, Six Sigma efforts offer business leaders a way to test the potential of people at all levels of the organization. These teams often have opportunities to meet with and present to senior management and show their ability to make positive change happen. You will, in short, be recognized for important work in a way unprecedented in the ordinary work-a-day world.

EXCITEMENT

Six Sigma is more fun than the kinds of success most people have had on the job in the past. With Six Sigma, you're taking on real issues that affect your ability to do good work, to understand how you contribute, and to make a difference. Corny as it may seem, a lot of people get pretty excited about that. We hope that you can, too. If those reasons aren't enough, perhaps you'll enjoy the reward of being part of a team, getting mugs and T-shirts, and sometimes even being given financial rewards.

ENLIGHTENMENT

A fourth E? This may be going a little far, but it's not impossible. Many people find that finally paying attention to the customer, process, and data is a breakthrough in their own way of looking at the world and addressing problems. Six Sigma can even help you deal with issues at home as you learn to ask better questions and make fact-based decisions.

SUMMARY

Six Sigma may mean extra work, but you can tap into a whole stable of benefits as well. Keep an open mind, learn, try new things, talk to new people, and have fun with what you may well find to be one of the most significant experiences in your career.

CHAPTER 6

A LOOK INSIDE THE SIX SIGMA TOOLKIT

In a way, any technique that helps you better understand, manage, and improve a business or a process can qualify as a Six Sigma tool. But some techniques are especially key tools in planning and executing Six Sigma projects. Understanding what those tools are will give you a clearer perspective on how Six Sigma works.

For convenience, we've grouped the tools into four categories. These categories aren't perfect; many tools can be used different ways. Our goal here is just a quick introduction. For more details and how-to information, you can look in a variety of other books, check out Web references, or just wait for your own Six Sigma training to begin.

TOOLS FOR GENERATING IDEAS AND ORGANIZING INFORMATION

BRAINSTORMING

Many Six Sigma methods have brainstorming, or idea generation, as a starting point. The basic purpose of brainstorming is to come up with a list of options for a task or a solution—usually a longer list that is shortened into a final choice. For example, a team may brainstorm which customers to interview or what questions to ask. Later, the team may use brainstorming again to list possible measures and still later to come up with creative improvement solutions.

A problem with brainstorming is that everybody thinks they are good at it. In fact, it takes work and discipline to be truly creative.

AFFINITY DIAGRAMMING

An affinity diagram is a grouping of ideas or options into categories. It's a common follow-up to brainstorming and helps synthesize and evaluate ideas. For example, after listing customers to interview, the team might "affinitize" its list into new, long-term, and lost customers.

Like brainstorming, affinity diagrams have several variations. The best method is for people to be quiet and to group ideas without speaking.

MULTIVOTING

Teams use multivoting to narrow down a list of ideas or options. It's also often used as a follow-up to brainstorming. Each participant gets a certain number of votes. The options getting the most votes overall are then given further analysis or consideration.

STRUCTURE TREE (TREE DIAGRAM)

A structure tree is used to show the links or hierarchy of the ideas brainstormed. Figure 6-1 shows how goals and possible solutions can be connected by using a structure tree. You might also use this approach to tie major customer needs, such as good value, to more specific requirements, such as low installation cost, low maintenance cost, and so on.

HIGH-LEVEL PROCESS MAP (SIPOC DIAGRAM)

SIPOC (pronounced "sye-pahk") is an acronym for Supplier, Input, Process, Output, Customer. SIPOC is used in the Define phase of DMAIC and is often a preferred method for diagramming major business processes and identifying possible measures.

The SIPOC diagram is used to show major activities, or subprocesses, in a business process, along with the framework of the process, represented by the Suppliers, Inputs, Outputs, and

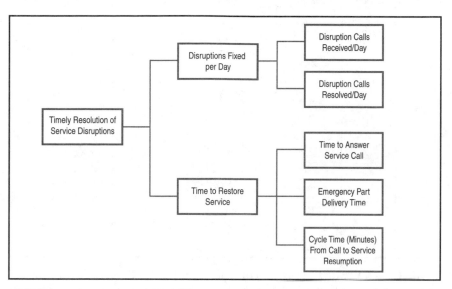

FIGURE 6-1. Structure Tree. There are many different ways to use this tool. (See a simple example, Figure 6-3.)

Customers. A SIPOC diagram is used to help define the boundaries and critical elements of a process without getting into so much detail that the big picture is lost. As you can see in Figure 6-2, the Process part of the diagram is represented by only a few high-level activities.

FLOWCHART (PROCESS MAP)

A flowchart is used to show details of a process, including tasks and procedures, alternative paths, decision points, and rework loops. A flowchart can be depicted as an "as-is" map showing a process as it currently works or as a "should-be" map showing how it ought to work. The level of detail will vary, depending on the objective. Many Black Belts now use software to draw their flowcharts but often start with a bunch of stickies on a wall. (See Figure 6-3.)

CAUSE-AND-EFFECT (FISHBONE) DIAGRAMS

A popular technique is the cause-and-effect, or fishbone or Ishikawa, diagram. In addition to having a lot of names, this tool borrows from other tools. The fishbone diagram (Figure 6-4) is

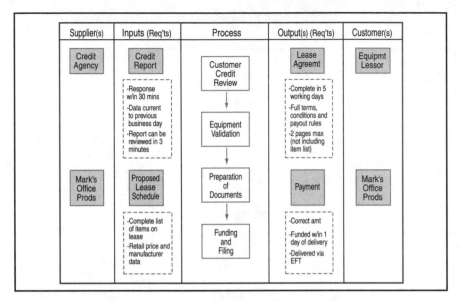

FIGURE 6-2. "SIPOC" Diagram of Equipment Leasing Process. This example shows "requirements" attached to each of the Inputs and Outputs (in dashed boxes).

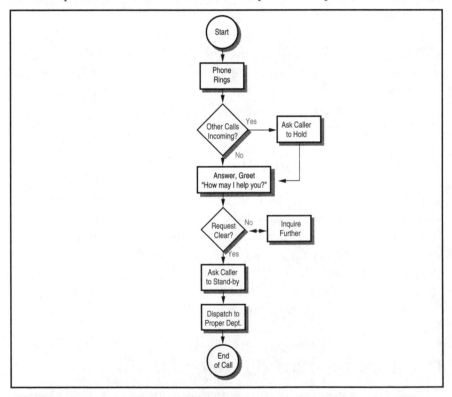

FIGURE 6-3. A Simple Flowchart or Process Map. Most business process flowcharts stick to four basic symbols: Circle—start and end of the process; Rectangle—task or activity; Diamond—decision or review point; Arrow—direction of the flow.

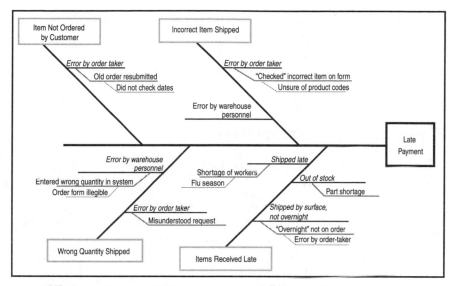

FIGURE 6-4. Cause and Effect or "Fishbone" Diagram. Cause categories (often called "major bones") are tailored to each situation.

used to brainstorm possible causes of a problem (or effect), and it puts the possible causes into groups, or affinities; causes that lead to other causes are linked as in a structure tree. The value of a cause-and-effect diagram is to help gather the collective ideas of a team on where a problem might arise and to help the team members think of all possible causes by clarifying major categories.

Cause-and-effect diagrams do not tell you the right cause. Rather, they help you develop educated guesses, or hypotheses, about where to focus measurement and further root cause analysis.

TOOLS FOR DATA GATHERING

SAMPLING

Counting everything that goes on in a process can be very expensive and a logistical nightmare. Luckily, as the pollsters will tell you, you can count a relatively few items and draw conclusions about all of them. (Okay, polls can be wrong, so you have to do sampling carefully). Sampling can save money and time and still give you excellent data to measure or to analyze a problem.

OPERATIONAL DEFINITIONS

Measurement is meaningless if people don't count and/or categorize things the same way. An operational definition is a clear, detailed, and understandable description of how to interpret data or events in your process, allowing you to gather data consistently and not end up with "apples and oranges." For example, in measuring "time waiting in line," an operational definition would tell you exactly when to start and stop the clock, thereby giving you data that is meaningful, not muddy.

VOICE OF THE CUSTOMER (VOC) METHODS

With customers as the focal point of much Six Sigma activity and objectives, the broad array of techniques that help an organization collect external customer input, assess and prioritize requirements, and provide ongoing feedback to the organization become critical. VOC tools include many simple and sophisticated market research methods, requirement analysis concepts, and newer technologies, such as data warehouses and data mining.

CHECKSHEETS AND SPREADSHEETS

Checksheets are forms used to collect and to organize data. Ideally, checksheets are designed by a Black Belt and/or team and have two key objectives:

1. To ensure that the right data is captured, with all necessary facts included, such as when it happened, how many, and what customer. We call these facts *stratification factors*.

2. To make data gathering as easy as possible for the collectors.

Checksheets can vary from simple tables and surveys to diagrams used to indicate where errors or damage occurred.

Spreadsheets are the place where checksheet data is collected and organized. A well-designed spreadsheet makes it much easier to use the data. Figure 6-5 shows a spreadsheet with data taken from observing patients eating new menu items in a hospital.

MEASUREMENT SYSTEMS ANALYSIS (MSA)

This big phrase covers a variety of methods used to make sure that measures are accurate and reliable. In Chapter 4, we noted that measurement itself can be a cause of issues in a process; MSA helps identify and weed out problems in the measures. For example, one MSA method is called Gage R & R (repeatability and reproducibility). This MSA method helps measure the effectiveness of gauges, rulers, and other measurement instru-

MENU ITEM	Portions Ordered	Portions Consumed	Percent Consumed
Asparagus	477	387	81.13%
Garlic Bits	255	12	4.71%
Chicken Nibbles	669	624	93.27%
Ice Cream Sundae	1121	1118	99.73%
Hot Dog Helper	235	124	52.77%
Spinach Thermador	112	21	18.75%
Onion Surprise	23	0	0.00%
Beef Brochette	611	544	89.03%
TOTALS	3503	2830	80.79%

FIGURE 6-5. Sample Spreadsheet. This one is simple; for extensive data the spreadsheets can be pretty complex.

ments. Checking on the people doing measures is a part of MSA as well.

TOOLS FOR PROCESS AND DATA ANALYSIS

PROCESS-FLOW ANALYSIS

Armed with a map or a flowchart of a key work process, you or a DMAIC team can start to scrutinize the process for redundancies, unclear hand-offs, unnecessary decision points, and so on. If you add in data about the process, other problems—delays, bottlenecks, defects, and rework—can also emerge. Process analysis can be one of the quickest ways to find clues about root causes of problems.

VALUE AND NON-VALUE-ADDED ANALYSIS

One big advantage of focusing attention on the requirements of external customers is the ability to assess processes based on value-added activities. Business processes tend to grow over time, and usually the added tasks—inspections, extra features, analysis, reports—turn out to have little or no benefit to people who pay the bills.

In value/non-value-added analysis, each step in a detailed process map is assessed on its real value to external customers. ("Would they pay us to do this?") It's never possible to eliminate all non-value-adding activities; some are in place to protect the business or to meet legal requirements. But this approach helps in what some of our clients have begun calling "atrocity removal": eliminating the dumb things that are unnecessary in a process and a drain on resources.

CHARTS AND GRAPHS: OVERVIEW

Usually, the first and best way to analyze measures of a process is to create a picture of the data. Charts and graphs are really nothing more than visual displays (pictures) of data. For most of us, looking at a pie chart or a line graph is a lot more meaningful and convenient than reading tables of numbers. And when you compare different segments of data—the stratification mentioned in the section on checksheets—you can make discoveries that the numbers themselves would hide.

For example, Figure 6-6(a) shows an initial pie chart covering the entire company, on reasons for complaints. Figure 6-5(b) and (c) show the same data broken out by region, giving you a very different picture. It's discoveries like this that help DMAIC teams both define their problems better and analyze the causes.

Charts and graphs are of various types, each offering a bit different picture of the data. A Black Belt will usually use at least a couple of these on a project. Following are some of the most commonly used types of charts and graphs.

Pareto Chart.   A Pareto is a specialized bar chart that breaks down a group by categories and compares them from largest to smallest. It's used to look for the biggest pieces of a problem or

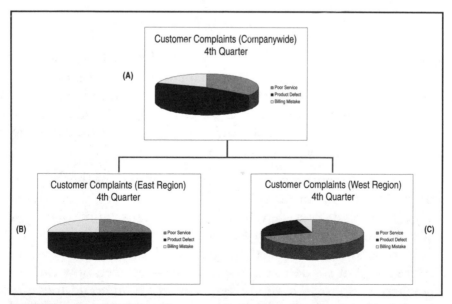

FIGURE 6-6.   Pie Charts. The two regional charts show detail that the full-company chart does not. This is an example of the value of "stratified" data.

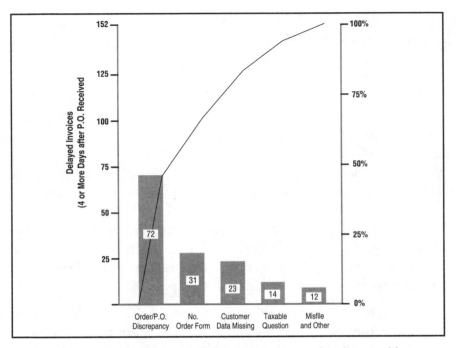

FIGURE 6-7. Pareto Chart. A DMAIC team looking at this chart would want to look deeper into the data before drawing any firm conclusions. It might, however, provide evidence favoring "orders" as being a key to the problem.

contributors to a cause. The Pareto chart (Figure 6-7) helps you figure out which of the few issues or problems have the most impact, so you can focus your project and solutions on those few, most impactful issues. The Pareto chart capitalizes on the so-called "80–20 Rule": Most of the problems (80) arise from relatively few causes (20).

Histogram (Frequency Plot). A histogram, another type of bar chart, shows the distribution or variation of data over a *range*: size, age, cost, length of time, weight, and so on. (A Pareto chart, by contrast, slices data by category.)

For instance, we know that a big chunk of our pizza deliveries are late, but we do not know how late—or even how early—they arrive. So, over several days or weeks, you could measure the time in minutes it takes to deliver pizzas to customers and then plot that data (see Figure 6-8).

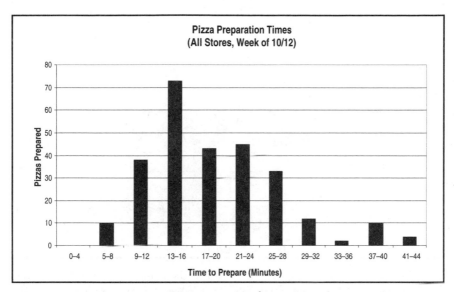

FIGURE 6-8. Histogram. The bars on this chart tell how long it took to prepare each pizza. Each bar represents a "range" and tells how many pizzas took the time within that range. For example, ten pizzas were prepared in from five to eight minutes.

In analyzing histograms, you can look for the shape of the bars or the curve, the width of the spread, or range, from top to bottom, or the number of "humps" in the bars. If you plot customer requirements on a histogram, you can quickly see how much of what you do is meeting—or not meeting—customers' needs.

Run (Trend) Chart. Pareto charts and histograms don't show you how things are changing over time. That's the job of a *run*, or *trend*, chart. Figure 6-9 shows the number of late pizzas per day over a month. (Noticing the Friday "spikes," which did not show up on the histogram (Figure 6-8) might make a Black Belt say,"Hmmm. . . .")

Scatter Plot (Correlation) Diagram. A Scatter plot looks for direct relationships between two factors in a process, usually to see whether they are correlated, meaning that a change in one is linked to a change in the other. If two measures show a relationship, one may be causing the other. However, that may not be true, so you have to be cautious about your conclusions.

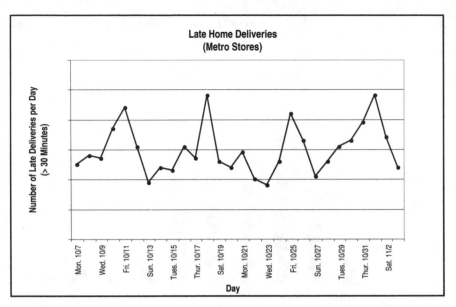

FIGURE 6-9. This Run or Trend Chart tracks the number of late home deliveries per day at Six Sigma Pizza. A possible "cycle" appears (a spike on Fridays), but the DMAIC team would need to investigate the data further.

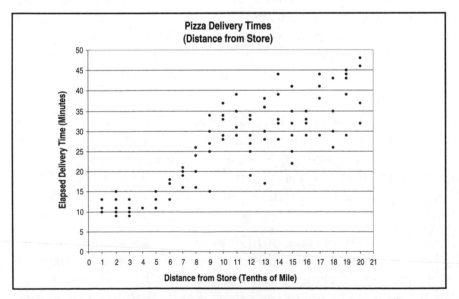

FIGURE 6-10. Scatter Plot showing relationship between distance and delivery time. This shows a "positive correlation" for city locations: the farther a driver has to travel, the longer a delivery is likely to take.

A BIT MORE DETAIL: SCATTER PLOTS, *Y*s AND *X*s

A scatter plot can help a DMAIC team see the relationship between the output, or *Y*, measures of a process and the input and process, or *X*, factors suspected of causing a problem. (See Chapter 4 for an explanation of *X* and *Y*.)

When a scatter plot is built, the suspected cause or influencing factor is plotted along the horizontal (*X*) axis of the graph. (Technically, this is called the independent variable and would correspond to a change in the process or input). The affected factor—often the problem or the output measure—is plotted on the vertical (*Y*) axis. (This is called the dependent variable because we suspect that it will change depending on a change in the *X* variable.)

If we see a clear correlation—a pattern of points and not just a "cloud"—it means that we're starting to understand the equation $Y = f(X)$. But DMAIC teams have to remember that just seeing correlation does not mean that the *X* is causing *Y*. The two may just change in tandem, based on other causes.

When an increase in one factor matches an increase in the other, as in Figure 6-10, it's called "positive correlation." When an increase in one matches a decrease in the other, it's called "negative correlation."

TOOLS FOR STATISTICAL ANALYSIS

Analyzing the process and digging into charts and graphs can often give a Black Belt everything needed to pinpoint the root cause of a problem. In many cases, though, the data is not clearcut, or you may need a level of proof beyond what visual tools can offer. In these cases, Six Sigma teams can apply more sophisticated *statistical analysis tools.*

The statistical part of the toolkit contains many different tools and formulas. Some of the broad families of statistical methods are

- *Tests of statistical significance.* These tools look for differences in groups of data to see whether they are meaningful.

A BIT MORE DETAIL: WHAT AND WHY "STATISTICS"?

In common terms, "statistics" just means "numbers," as in "First-quarter statistics show the Hogs gained 110 yards passing." When we refer to statistical analysis tools, we're referring to a group of methods and formulas that help us draw conclusions from the numbers.

Some of the tools help us determine whether what we think we see in the data is really true. For example, it may look as though we get more pizza orders on Fridays than on any other day of the week. A statistical test will give a more precise answer as to whether the Friday spike is real. (If it's real, we'd say that it's "statistically significant.") Other statistics can be used to help predict what's going to happen in the future in certain circumstances.

Statistical analysis tools are based on fundamental laws of probability (the coin toss and dice-rolling science). In this analysis, we always start with the assumption that everything we observe is simply the result of random chance. When statistical tests show that the results are not random, you can say "Ah-ha!"

A good thing about statistical analysis is that we always assume that our suspicions are wrong (a "null hypothesis"). If we turn out to not be wrong, the result has a lot more credibility.

A not-so-good thing about statistics is that the answers are still not always black and white, but they are certainly a lot more reliable than guesswork or opinion! That's why statistical tools are a great complement to the fact-based approach we take in Six Sigma.

These tests include Chi-square, *t*-tests, and analysis of variance (ANOVA).

- *Correlation and regression.* These tools, which are akin to a scatter plot but can get a lot more complex, include regression coefficients, simple linear regression, multiple regression, surface response tests, and so on. These tools test for the presence, strength, and nature of the links among variables in a process or a product, such as how tire pressure, temperature, and speed would affect gas mileage.

- *Design of experiments.* DOE is a collection of methods for developing and conducting controlled assessments of how a process or a product performs, usually testing two or more characteristics under different conditions. In addition to helping target causes of a problem, DOE can be essential to get maximum benefit out of solutions (called "optimizing" results).

If you took statistics in school or have a chance to use stats from time to time, you probably recognize some of these tools. Remember that if you are asked to participate in a Six Sigma project, you'll be given training in these tools, and no one will expect you to be an expert in them right away.

TOOLS FOR IMPLEMENTATION AND PROCESS MANAGEMENT

Project Management Methods.   Just because you can analyze a problem, it doesn't mean that you can put a solution in place. Six Sigma companies recognize early on the importance of strong project management skills: planning, budgeting, scheduling, communication, people management. Technical project management tools (Gantt charts or timelines, for example) are also important.

Potential Problem Analysis and Failure Mode and Effects Analysis.   These are two of the key problem-prevention methods that are applied both in implementing new processes and in running them every day. Both start with listing (brainstorming) the many things that could go wrong. Then, the potential problems are prioritized. Finally, the biggest risks are protected by looking for ways to prevent them from happening, as well as ways to limit the damage if they do occur (called "contingencies").

Stakeholder Analysis.   Complex change can affect a lot of people. Savvy teams or leaders recognize that they can hope for change to be successful only if they consider the needs and perspectives of the various parties involved: the stakeholders. Stakeholder analysis involves identifying the people and groups that need to be considered, their likely views on the project or solution, and approaches to gaining their input and/or support.

Force Field Diagram.   A force field (Figure 6-11) shows the relationship between factors that help promote a change and those that oppose or create resistance to it. Like stakeholder analysis, the force field is used to develop plans to build support for a critical change. (Usually, the best strategy is to concentrate on weakening the resisting forces through education or refinements to the solution.)

Process Documentation.   As a DMAIC project reaches conclusion—with solutions in place and results in hand—the time comes to turn over responsibility to those who will manage the process on an ongoing basis. Creating effective, clear, not overly complex process documentation—process maps, task instructions, measures, and so on—is the last and most important element of the DMAIC Control step.

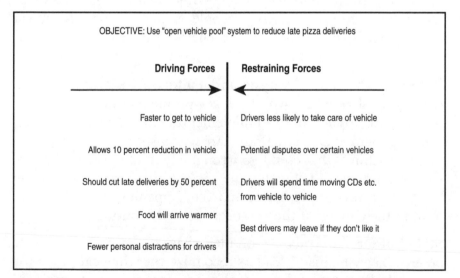

FIGURE 6-11.   This Force Field analysis chart helps a team identify the factors supporting (Driving) or opposing (Restraining) a proposed solution. Every change will have some factors working against it; Six Sigma teams must find ways to make their ideas acceptable and workable for as many people as possible.

Balanced Scorecards and Process Dashboards.   Six Sigma has placed new attention on the ability of people throughout an organization to keep tabs on current performance, trends, and issues on key indicators in a process. Balanced scorecards and process dashboards provide a summary of critical measures that, ideally, give real-time feedback and promote prompt attention to issues and opportunities. These tools typically feature both output (Y) and process and input (X) measures and go well beyond traditional financial data.

SUMMARY

As you can tell from just a quick scan through this chapter, Six Sigma is rich with tools that help people make better decisions, solve problems, and manage change. But beware of assuming that Six Sigma and the tools are one and the same. Using too many tools, making them too complicated, or demanding they be used when they aren't helpful can undermine the goals of Six Sigma just as easily as not using tools. We'll wrap up with these tips for Six Sigma tool users:

- Use only the tools that help you get the job done
- Keep it as simple as possible
- When a tool isn't helping, stop and try something else

CHAPTER 7

SIX SIGMA IN ACTION:

SOME SUCCESS STORIES

One of the best ways to get a sense of the power of Six Sigma is to see some of the problems and opportunities that have been addressed by applying the tools and some creative thinking.

CASE 1: REPAIRING REPAIRS

A major appliance repair organization recognized the need to improve its ability to return items to customers when promised. Too often, repairs were late and customers disappointed when they would call or drop by to pick up their VCR, lawn mower, or computer.

A multi-level DMAIC team narrowed their scope to two repair locations and carefully analyzed all the causes of late repairs. One of their discoveries: that the time taken to repair a product was only part of the trouble. The time to ship appliances back and forth from repair shop to customer site also was a big contributor to missed dates.

Based on its findings and cost/benefit analysis, the team and colleagues in the two pilot facilities implemented several changes to streamline the process and increase the number of appliances returned to customers when promised.

CASE 2: SIX SIGMA IN SPACE

A provider of satellite communication links found itself facing customer complaints and a business opportunity. Most of the company's customers purchased long-term contracts for dedicated up- and down-links. (For example, banks use satellites to send transaction data around the country.) Other potential customers wanted only short-time connections, perhaps for a global videoconference or TV news report.

The problem was, it took just as much time to approve a contract for short connections as for the long deals. The result was that customers asking for the short-time satellite services were upset, and the company was losing business.

A Six Sigma improvement team, led by a staff attorney, used the DMAIC process to define, measure, and analyze the contracting process. Old assumptions on how much scrutiny was needed for a contract had to be changed, and new, streamlined procedures put in place and tested.

The company made the contracting process faster and more customer friendly. As a result, the company not only had happier customers but also boosted its business, with a total benefit of about $1 million a year.

CASE 3: CANCEL THAT NEW PLANT

With a highly successful new pain-killing drug, a pharmaceutical company launched plans to build a $200 million production facility to double its capacity. As that effort was getting started, some new participants in the firm's Six Sigma effort decided to investigate some short-term steps to boost production in the existing plant. In their data collection, the participants first discovered that only about 40 percent of the drug being packaged was usable. Looking further, they learned that the sealing method for the drug vials was so inconsistent that some would not be completely closed, whereas others were too long to fit in the box.

The team used several rounds of testing and refining the sealing process (using "design of experiments" methods) and determined the best combination of factors—temperature, time, distance, and so on—to ensure a good seal. With these changes and a few $50 parts to regulate the sealing equipment, the team quickly boosted yields in the plant to 85 percent. The increased capacity eliminated the need for the new plant (!) and set the stage for further improvements in the production-line yields.

CASE 4: GETTING PAID, ON TIME

A large computer company used a phone center operation to handle orders for fairly routine parts and supplies. Although sales were good and customers seemed mostly happy, the company was suffering: More than 12 percent of payments due from customers were more than 90 days past due.

The "traditional" approach would be to send collectors after the customers, but this firm's finance group decided to apply a DMAIC analysis to the problem. An early step, getting Voice of the Customer input, revealed that customers were not so happy. In particular, those with overdue bills claimed that because the orders they'd been invoiced for were wrong, sent to the wrong place, or had other problems, they were not going to pay.

That initial cause—mistakes in orders—led to another question: Why were so many orders wrong? Deeper analysis traced the issue to an unsuspected source: Phone representatives, who were rewarded on the number of calls they handled, were taking complex orders so quickly that the orders themselves were inaccurate. The real cause, it seemed, was a short-sighted incentive system.

The group tested its solution with a pilot team of order takers, who were given a new set of performance guidelines that included both productivity—number of calls handled—and order accuracy. In the one-month test, the pilot group showed an 80 percent decrease in order errors!

Implementing this solution, the group was able to cut late payments in half. In addition, it eliminated a big source of defects impacting key customers.

CASE 5: RIGHT TECH, RIGHT CALL

The appliance repair company mentioned earlier (see Case One) suffered a long-term problem: When parts had to be ordered for a repair made at a customer's home, it was usually a different technician sent back with the part. This caused problems for both the company and the customer, for example:

- The new technician was not familiar with the problem
- The customer was surprised to see a different technician
- Significant "rework" would be done, costing the customer time and the company money
- Technicians were frustrated by not being able to complete a job they'd started.

In a significant number of cases, three or four technician visits would be required to repair the problem—a real aggravation for someone whose washer is on the fritz.

The solution was fairly simple: a logic change in the technician scheduling software increased the number of cases in which the same repair technician is routed back to his or her original customer. Knowing the situation and with the right part, "First Time Complete" repair calls increased significantly.

CASE 6: IMPROVING LOAN QUALITY

A leading mortgage lender was suffering from a wave of rework. In spite of a strong mortgage market, the company was stuck with a pile of newly closed loans with defects—errors in documents, terms, conditions, and so on—that made them unsellable. (Most mortgage companies sell the loans they write to large, quasi-government corporations, such as Fannie Mae and Freddie Mac.) The stack of defective—unsold—mortgages meant that the company's money was tied up and could not be used to lend to other people.

A Six Sigma Black Belt and several Green Belts first examined all the reasons why loans were "in limbo." The team identified eight major reasons the loans were unsellable and focused on solutions for the top reasons. Over a few months, the team was able to cut the pile of unsold loans in half, saving the company nearly $150 million. Further projects—including some process-redesign efforts—helped eliminate other causes of defective loans, so the company could use its capital more efficiently and keep more customers happy.

CASE 7: CLOSING THE HOOD

An automobile manufacturer used Six Sigma VOC methods to identify and to prioritize issues noted by its customers. One of the problems discovered on a top-selling model was a surprise: Vehicle owners, on average, had to raise the hood nearly a foot or more and let it fall with a lot of force just to get it to close. Although the hood did close properly, it was clearly an annoyance to customers and warranted attention.

Examining data on production of the hood, the Six Sigma Black Belt was able to find inconsistencies in the manufacturing of the latch parts and assembly. Redefining and controlling variation in the production process eliminated the problem. Now the hood will close if you drop it from just a few inches. The cost savings to the company were not great, but the project eliminated a key source of customer dissatisfaction with a car that owners otherwise love!

SUMMARY

This sampling of Six Sigma projects represents a tiny fraction of all the improvements and changes to processes going on throughout the world. Some people ask, "Wouldn't these problems have been solved anyway?" And the answer is, "Some might have."

But in many cases, it's likely that the approach taken would not have led to the powerful solutions we see here, where customer needs, process knowledge, and data drive the effort. And it's certain that without the energy Six Sigma is prompting companies to apply to identifying their key problems (not to mention fixing them), many of the projects being tackled by Six Sigma teams would not have been addressed at all.

CHAPTER 8

A NOTE TO MANAGERS:

How You Can Help Lead Six Sigma

Throughout this book, we've assumed that your role would most likely be one of a participant rather than a leader of the initiative in your organization. Now it's time to admit that no Six Sigma effort will truly transform an organization—or even achieve significant successes—without leaders throughout the business. Senior managers have to be on board and play an active role, but their will alone won't make the concepts and tools we've described take root.

This chapter is for those people who manage and guide from the departments, divisions, branch offices, subsidiaries: middle management. Our goal is to help you effectively contribute to Six Sigma and do the right things to make it work well for you and your people, as well as for the entire company.

THE CHALLENGE TO LEADERS AT ALL LEVELS

A common, understandable response some middle managers have to news of a Six Sigma initiative is "Oh, no!" Like other business initiatives you've likely experienced, you can rightly guess at some of the things in store for you and your people:

- More work
- New, different priorities
- Demands on time for meetings, planning, training, projects

- The need to work as a team with other groups
- Plans that will change and then change again and maybe again

Six Sigma can be disruptive, confusing, and difficult to explain to your people. You could decide to just ignore it altogether and hope that it will go away, or maybe pretend that you're behind Six Sigma but mostly just go through the motions. Or you could work against Six Sigma and try to convince your colleagues to help you kill it.

Doing so is potentially risky (to your long-term employment, in particular). More important, it doesn't do you the favor of trying to make Six Sigma work for you, in spite of the challenges it poses.

THE POTENTIAL BENEFITS TO LEADERS AT ALL LEVELS

Leaders throughout a company have a lot to gain through Six Sigma. Following are some of the "biggies":

- *Clearer priorities.* One of the fairly early effects of launching Six Sigma projects is the realization that the 500 separate projects going on in the business are too much. To rally resources to DMAIC projects, most companies recognize that they have to cut out some of the trivial things they're working on. If one of your pet projects gets halted, that's a drag. But the benefit is usually more focus on fewer, more critical initiatives.

- *Fewer conflicts: more teamwork.* If you're like most managers, the majority of problems you deal with come from confusion or disconnects with other groups in the business. Six Sigma gives you a forum to better understand and manage those hand-offs by understanding the "big picture" of an end-to-end process. Better teamwork is often driven by a realignment of goals, so each group is working toward the same results.

- *Better, more useful data.* Six Sigma will help you reassess the measures you use to make decisions, solve problems, and evaluate people. The result is often more meaningful data tied to real customer requirements, costs, and defects.

- *Development for your people.* Six Sigma training, at all levels, gives people a range of new skills and a new focus on smarter ways to do business. If you have bright, high-potential people in your ranks, Six Sigma can be a great way to give them new challenges and an opportunity to be recognized and rewarded.

- *Improved resources, energy, and results.* Along with the extra work Six Sigma may demand of you and your people is an opportunity to make critical changes in your processes and performance. Improving performance is fun and exciting.

Whether you are a first-line supervisor, a department head, or a group VP, to achieve these benefits requires your participation in listening, questioning, giving feedback, and communicating priorities. Six Sigma does demand leaders who can exercise judgment, take risks, make some tough calls, and exert influence even when they don't have direct control.

If there is a single word that describes your most important contribution, it's *involvement*. Being involved with the Six Sigma effort—helping Black Belts and teams with their problems, providing resources and information to the best of your ability, breaking down barriers, and confronting issues honestly—will contribute to the overall success of the program and likely to your success, too!

MEETING THE CHALLENGES TO ACHIEVE THE BENEFITS

From a practical standpoint, you can't achieve the benefits we've outlined without some sacrifice. Here are some key questions that leaders top to bottom often pose about Six Sigma and some key points for dealing with them:

"One (or more) of my key people is being assigned to a Six Sigma project. How can I handle it?" The situation involves two issues:

1. *"Losing" a Black Belt.* Because this is usually a full-time role—and you may not be able to "backfill"—you're going to have to absorb the reduction as best you can. If the Black Belt's project falls in your area, that should soften the blow: The results will often boost efficiency, reducing your need for the "extra body."

2. *Contributing team members/Green Belts.* These are part-time assignments but can definitely put pressure on your area.

   Some tips:

- Work with the Black Belt to help coordinate times for meetings and to minimize impact on your ongoing operations.
- Keep track of the progress of the team so that you can anticipate your employee's involvement and time demands.
- Enlist the ideas and help of others in your group to work around the time the team member will be busy or absent (this involves them in Six Sigma).
- Work with other leaders to share limited resources.
- Make use of overtime and other fill-in opportunities.

The most important thing not to do is ignore your people's Six Sigma assignment and pull them away from those responsibilities. This not only puts the team members in a bind but also will drag out the DMAIC project so they're just away longer than planned!

"I'm being asked for Six Sigma project ideas. What should I be looking for?" Finding and selecting good projects is one of the keys to getting results from Six Sigma and one of the toughest things to do right. Here's how to ensure that your ideas are a good fit:

- Identify a specific, observable problem with a measurable impact. "Sales of widgets are off 20 percent" is fine. "Salespeople aren't getting enough training" is not.
- Don't include a solution or a cause in your project proposal. This is a lot more difficult than it sounds. If your project description includes "things we might do" or "reasons why this is a problem," you're probably breaking this rule, and it happens a lot.
- Avoid your pet projects. You may be tempted to sic a Black Belt or a Green Belt on some of the annoying issues you've just never had time for. Cleaning up the database or setting up a vendor review may be good things to do, but you don't need DMAIC to get them done.
- Keep in mind the two Ms: meaningful and manageable. A Six Sigma project should offer significant benefits; there should be little debate about why it's important. Choosing a "world hunger" project ("Communication with customers is horrible") will overwhelm a team and create either a long project or just plain failure. Look for ways to slice each project into workable pieces that would contribute to solving the larger issue ("Northeast customers are not receiving e-mail updates on time").

"I volunteered to be a Champion for a DMAIC project, but what am I supposed to be doing?" We noted earlier that Champions are often a weakness in the Six Sigma list of responsibilities. A few common sense tips can help you be a more effective Champion.

- *Take your role seriously.* Your contribution can easily make a difference between a successful or an unsuccessful DMAIC project; it's not just a figurehead role.
- *Create a "contract" with your Black Belt.* Agree up-front on how you will communicate, how actively you'll get

involved in the team's work, what format you'll use for
project tollgate reviews, and so on.

- *Offer suggestions, not criticism.* Remember that a project team
  is often learning Six Sigma skills and applying them to tough
  issues. Your advice and counsel, presented well, should be
  welcome; attacks on the team's mental capacity won't.

- *Devote the time and keep commitments.* The Champion's
  responsibilities are usually not a huge time drain. But the
  role does need to be high on your agenda, not the first
  thing to get knocked off when pressures arise.

- *Abandon your assumptions.* One of the most frustrating
  events for a Black Belt or a team is when a leader looks at
  the data that has been gathered and swears, "This can't be
  true!" It can be a shock to find out that your long-held
  beliefs are not true, but it's a common phenomenon that
  you should be prepared for in Six Sigma.

**"All managers are being asked to identify key "output"
measures for their processes, but where do I start?"**   The
easy answer is, "With the customer(s) of your process and the
products, services, and information you provide them." If you
can refine your understanding of their requirements, you'll be
much better equipped to define your output (Y) measures. You
may want to negotiate with your customers as you clarify their
requirements. (Sometimes they ask for things that aren't important or miss things that are.) And you want to test all the
requirements to ensure that they connect with real, external
customer needs.

Otherwise, this task is often much simpler than managers
expect.

**"My people are being asked to collect data and are com-
plaining about it. Now what?"**   This is an opportunity to use
your change-leadership skills in connection with Six Sigma.
Here are some steps to address these situations.

1. *Investigate.* Try to find out what's really being asked of your
   people. Are the instructions clear? Is the request as big a

hassle as they claim? Have the objectives been explained? Are people being targeted, or is the process?

2. *Communicate with the Black Belt.* If the measurement request is really tough, you may need to go back to the DMAIC team to see whether its goals or data collection process can be adjusted. You may also want to ask for clearer objectives and/or assurances to help people feel comfortable about their "anonymity" in the measurement.

3. *Communicate with and encourage your people.* You owe it to your staff to make their data gathering as easy, or nondisruptive, as possible. You also owe it to your colleagues working on a Six Sigma project to help them get the data they need. Once you are comfortable that the plan is reasonable, your best strategy is to support the measurement effort and do what you can to ensure that the data is collected accurately and communicated promptly.

SUPPORTING IMPROVEMENT OF SIX SIGMA

In encouraging you to support the Six Sigma effort, we are not suggesting that leaders throughout the business show blind faith. We have seen quite a few instances in which middle managers and supervisors have helped enhance an initiative through constructive criticism. We have also seen plenty of others in which they were reluctant to point out flaws in the plan.

The people who guide the Six Sigma effort in your organization should look for input from you and your peers. And you should be prepared to present issues and to offer suggestions, which overall should improve the effectiveness of Six Sigma.

As a leader, you can take a leadership role in Six Sigma or wait and see what happens. A proactive stance is usually the best course for you and for the company.

CHAPTER 9

A NOTE TO SIX SIGMA EMPLOYEES:

NINE THINGS YOU SHOULD DO AND FIVE SKILLS TO DEVELOP

If Six Sigma has arrived or is on the horizon at your organization, you can expect some changes and opportunities to come your way. Beyond understanding what Six Sigma is you need to understand how you can make Six Sigma a positive experience. So here are some tips and hints that will make you better prepared to thrive in a Six Sigma organization.

NINE THINGS YOU SHOULD DO

1. *Learn the goals and objectives of the Six Sigma effort.* Each company has a somewhat different perspective on why Six Sigma is needed and what it will help achieve. Listen and look for communications about the initiative's vision, plans for teams and training, scale and speed, and roles and responsibilities. All this will help you anticipate what you can do—or what you'll be asked to do—to contribute to the Six Sigma change.

2. *Prepare for some confusion.* Six Sigma may be a goal of near perfect performance, but implementing Six Sigma in a business is never perfect. Instead, you can expect plans to change, roles to evolve, signals to get crossed, and projects to be launched and revamped or abandoned.

This is all a part of the messy job of organization change. Perhaps in your company, the messiness will be kept to a minimum, but some of it is inevitable, and you should not let it discourage you from benefiting from the good parts of change.

3. *Begin looking at your work from a SIPOC point of view.* You can get a head start on practicing the concepts of Six Sigma if you think of your job as part of a chain of activities: suppliers and inputs (the things you rely on), process (the work you and your colleagues do), and outputs and customers (the final product and the people who receive it).

Start asking yourself some important questions: "Do I understand what my/our customers really need? (And do they?) How well are we meeting their needs? Is our process well organized and efficient, or is it confused and rework-ridden? How well have we conveyed our needs to suppliers?" (Remember, these may be people in your company.)

This analysis does not have to be detailed, but it may give you ideas for Six Sigma projects. It may also give you a chance to see how Six Sigma principles can make your life easier and your job more productive.

4. *Take advantage of learning opportunities.* Six Sigma training can be challenging, but it's also full of great ideas and tools that can help you in your daily life, as well as at work. Although we, and others, tend to emphasize the techniques you learn in Six Sigma, it's true that a lot of what you learn are better ways to apply plain old common sense thinking. (Common sense, we've heard and remarked, is often the least common of the senses.) So if you get a chance to be involved in awareness training or Green Belt courses, or even to become a Black Belt, your best bet is to go into it expecting to work hard and gain a lot.

5. *Avoid paranoia.* One of the biggest hindrances to success in Six Sigma—for an individual or a business—comes from fear and worry. Sometimes, it's just fear of change; in other

cases, it's worry that you will be blamed for problems being analyzed. It can even happen that Black Belts or DMAIC teams will be afraid to tell their project Champions, "Hey! This project you've assigned us is too big!"

We've not heard of anyone being reprimanded, demoted, or fired for issues that arise from Six Sigma projects or from providing honest, constructive feedback on the Six Sigma initiative. (If it has happened, it's mighty rare.) If you look at this as a positive opportunity to make things better, it has a much greater chance of success than if you approach Six Sigma like the third rail on the subway tracks.

6. *Expect changes and challenges to come.* When we say to avoid fear and paranoia, we don't mean that you should not anticipate some disruptions and challenges. As we've described, participating in a Six Sigma project usually requires some sacrifice.

Adopting new procedures and living by new processes is difficult if you are comfortable with the way you've always done things. Changes may even mean people being reassigned or given brand-new roles. And, yes, sometimes Six Sigma projects lead to people being laid off—it's one of the ways a company can be more efficient. Usually, however, those most painful changes are made for good reasons, not just as some blind effort to save money. So even Six Sigma "headcount reductions," painful though they may be, are usually less of a challenge than other staff cuts.

7. *Take responsibility for your own learning.* We use this phrase a lot in training programs. It's not a trainer's cop-out, though. It simply means, "Be proactive in finding out what you need and want to know." Asking questions, reading books and articles, talking to people involved in Six Sigma teams, attending informational meetings, using chat rooms or e-mail contacts: These should all be part of your effort to learn and understand more about Six Sigma. Remember, some answers will be tentative, but there are few organizations in which you can't learn more if you try.

8. *Volunteer, be patient, and don't get discouraged.* Sounds like a mix of suggestions, doesn't it? But these are related: First, if you feel eager, ready, and enthusiastic about getting actively involved in Six Sigma efforts, let your manager or other key people know. If you have project ideas, send them along. On the other hand, remember that your company or division may have more participants than it can handle, so your offer may not lead to immediate assignment to a DMAIC team. Even the most aggressive Six Sigma roll-outs can't get everyone involved right away. So if you are only on the outskirts of Six Sigma for a while, hang in there.

9. *Be ready for the long haul!* Companies let past improvement initiatives dwindle away because they never really became ingrained in the management processes. Six Sigma holds the promise of being really different. As the leader of one of our clients put it recently: "As we go along, the more I realize the value of Six Sigma is not just in projects but even more in how it improves the way we think and manage the business." Six Sigma is certain to evolve, but based on the results and impacts it's achieved so far, it seems likely to be around for quite a while.

FIVE SKILLS TO DEVELOP

The skills you will need to participate successfully in Six Sigma are not on the level of neurosurgery. Here are the five biggies:

1. *The ability to see the "big picture."* Being an expert in your own field or job role is fine. But Six Sigma performance relies on people who can see and understand a process from end to end. So-called empowered people in a Six Sigma company are those with the broader view and the ability to make decisions based on what works for the end customer and the whole process.

2. *The ability to gather data.* Gathering data does not mean statistical wizardry. It's about being able to separate factual

observation from opinion and guess and to record or explain the facts accurately.

There's an old saying: "In God we trust; all others bring data." It's going to be even more true in a Six Sigma world.

3. *The ability to break through old assumptions.* The biggest unseen obstacles to improving your business are probably the current beliefs on such things as "what our customers care about"; "how important this task is"; "that's something we could never afford"; or "we have the best process in the industry."

Many of these kinds of statements turn out to be wrong. Holding on to these beliefs freezes change and invites complacency. Today, complacency in business is frequently a terminal disease.

4. *The ability to work collaboratively.* Six Sigma projects and results have repeatedly proved that a win-win approach creates more value for everyone than does a win-lose approach. Along with the ability to see the big picture, you'll have to be comfortable with using that understanding to find better ways to team up, share, take responsibility, listen, value other opinions, and develop solutions that work for the greatest benefit—usually starting with benefits to external customers. This is what GE Chairman Jack Welch has called a "boundaryless" organization.

5. *The ability to thrive on change.* Change will happen whether you like it or not. Change for no good reason is bad, of course, but change that makes you and your coworkers better able to get the right things done is terrific. The most important skill overall in Six Sigma is just that: making change work for you, your customers and your organization.

There are no simple ways to develop these five key skills. Most of them start with your attitude. We hope that in the lessons you've learned in *What Is Six Sigma?* you can feel the sense of optimism and energy we see in the companies in which Six Sigma is making an impact. If you do, you'll be starting with the right attitude for you to learn these skills, too.

FINAL NOTE

You might think that after working with Six Sigma tools and concepts for years, we'd finally have all the answers. The truth (and fun) of it, however, is that we never stop getting new insights and ideas. We'd encourage you, our readers and customers, to share your insights or questions. You can contact us by e-mail at wiss@pivotalresources.com, We hope to hear of your successes!

APPENDIX

YIELD (%)	DPMO	Sigma
6.68	933200	0
8.455	915450	0.125
10.56	894400	0.25
13.03	869700	0.375
15.87	841300	0.5
19.08	809200	0.625
22.66	773400	0.75
26.595	734050	0.875
30.85	**691500**	**1**
35.435	645650	1.125
40.13	598700	1.25
45.025	549750	1.375
50	500000	1.5
54.975	450250	1.625
59.87	401300	1.75
64.565	354350	1.875
69.15	**308500**	**2**
73.405	265950	2.125
77.34	226600	2.25
80.92	190800	2.375
84.13	158700	2.5
86.97	130300	2.625
89.44	105600	2.75
91.545	84550	2.875
93.32	**66800**	**3**
94.79	52100	3.125
95.99	40100	3.25
96.96	30400	3.375
97.73	22700	3.5
98.32	16800	3.625
98.78	12200	3.75
99.12	8800	3.875
99.38	**6200**	**4**
99.565	4350	4.125
99.7	3000	4.25
99.795	2050	4.375
99.87	1300	4.5
99.91	900	4.625
99.94	600	4.75
99.96	400	4.875
99.977	**230**	**5**
99.982	180	5.125
99.987	130	5.25
99.992	80	5.375
99.997	30	5.5
99.99767	23.35	5.625
99.99833	16.7	5.75
99.999	10.05	5.875
99.99966	**3.4**	**6**

FIGURE A-1. Sigma capability conversion table